Scottish Story

A coming of age in the town of Arbroath.

J.H. WILSON

A Scottish Story

CreateSpace

First Edition (Dec 2012)
Second Edition (Jan 2013)

J.H.Wilson
scotimp@hotmail.com

ISBN-13: 9781481043137
ISBN-10:1481043137

©GraphicMaps.com
Atlantic Ocean
Orkney Islands
Shetland Islands
Pentland Firth
North Sea
Thurso
Kirkwall
Stornoway
Wick
Lewis
The Minch
Northern Highlands
SCOTLAND
LOW / HILLS / MOUNTAINS
Outer Hebrides
Moray Firth
Skye
Peterhead
Loch Ness
Inverness
Inner Hebrides
Grampian Mts.
Aberdeen
Fort William
Scotland
50 mi
50 km
Sea of the Hebrides
Ben Nevis
Dundee
Arbroath
Perth
St. Andrews
Mull
Central Lowlands
Firth of Forth
Stirling
Jura
Kirkcaldy
Glasgow
Edinburgh
Tweed River
Islay
Clyde River
Loch Lomond
Ayr
Southern Uplands
Cheviot Hills
Ireland
Arran
Northern Ireland
North Channel
Dumfries
CLICK HERE FOR LARGER MAP
England
Belfast
Stranraer

Contents

Foreword

This collection of memories is intended to portray Arbroath and related topics from 1938 through 1953. I've written this as I remember it, no frills but some mild understatement. A number of events, people and places to which I refer, are captured in "Wir Bookie" and "Wir Other Bookie" from the files of the Arbroath Herald. Some of the material and photographs are not of the best quality but you go with what you've got.

My wife of 50 years, Violet and our three daughters, Wendy, Laura and Claire are all Arbroath born. California residents for thirty years their memories of Arbroath are very different from mine.

Introduction

The early morning train to Dundee was late. I turned up the collar of my coat against the wind. Scotland can be cold in early October. Now with my brother laid to rest beside my mother and grandmother I had time to think about my return flight to San Francisco. However as I paced the empty platform I was unable to focus on the present.

The realization that I would never be able to talk to my brother Willie again triggered thoughts of my youth. The old iron railings atop the high bank overlooking the platforms still stood guard. As small boys we had often jammed our heads through those railings watching iron behemoths belching steam and soot, racing by on shiny rails that led to places unknown to us.

My slow walk up the West Port to the railway station took me past my old newsagent's shop, it was derelict. Mathieson's grocer's shop where I got my first "message bike" was now a second hand clothing store. No greeting or acknowledgement from the odd passerby, a stranger in the town of my birth.

Willie, my mother and grandmother last stood together on this very platform fifty years ago to the month. They came to say goodbye to a fresh faced fifteen year old, leaving for a new life in the Royal Air Force.

How long is that train going to be ….?

Arbroath

If Hollywood's Braveheart, William Wallace or Robert the Bruce had returned to Arbroath in the late 1930's, they would have found the Abbey in better shape than when they last saw it. The population would be larger, the fishing boats would be smaller and horses would still be working the streets. Like many others before me I didn't appreciate the town's history until after I left. My town was a playground of balls and beaches not artifacts and Abbey's.

The weather was normally sunny but rarely hot. Should the temperature exceed seventy degrees for more than three consecutive days it was considered to be a heat wave. Tourism was a major industry. The town boasted that it had "the most sunshine in Scotland." What they didn't tell you was that the wind blew continually and what passed for a suntan might just as easily be attributed to being weather beaten! The big city holidaymakers, Glaswegians mostly didn't seem to care. They filled the Bed and Breakfasts and rented tiny caravans, rain or shine. Just as well because they could depend on getting both!

The towns engineering skills were rooted in the industries of the early 1800's. Mills still imported flax from India. Sails were no longer required but tarpaulins and other hardwearing waterproof coverings were. Gerrard Brothers shipyard was repairing and building wooden fishing vessels on a limited scale. The exporting of herring to the Baltic had been replaced by the exporting of Angus cattle. A more tangible export was the young men and women who left the town for all corners of what was then called The British Empire. Keith & Blackman and Fraser's were the pre-eminent mechanical engineering companies.

The fishing community resided at the "fit o the toon." They were as self-sufficient a community as it was possible to be. They exemplified the closeness of a group who lived hard lives and shared a dangerous way of earning a living. The sea's bounty helped the town prosper, its anger brought disasters and acts of bravery that typified the best of human character. Boat's left the harbor at four am on the morning tide, returning by mid-afternoon. The sandstone harbor and seawall provided protection for over forty such boats.

Catches were auctioned daily on the quay. Each boat had that special box, a mixture of fish that didn't meet the standard catch. I loved the excitement of waiting to see what exotic creature might just show up in that box. I never did understand the nods; gestures and expressions, which helped, decide price and ownership. White labels marked Swankie, Pert, Spink, Cargill, Beattie or Smith decreed the winning bidder. Paper labels stick to wet fish readily. Bye names such as "Darkie," "Bets" or "Eck" were often used to identify a buyer with a popular family name. Fish landed at three in the afternoon were gutted, filleted and sold by four. Served with chips, bread and butter it was on the tea table by 5 o'clock.

The agricultural community was just as strong and equally as independent as the "fisher fowk." Farming was very labor-intensive with many families, living and working on the land, mostly on small farms. Farm workers children, either walked or rode a bicycle to school regardless of the weather. There was no school bus. Rosy cheeks, clipped conversation and a measured gait were hallmarks of those who worked and lived on the land. Never a pace or word wasted. On the farm bachelors stayed in the "bothy," a communal dwelling where single men shared limited home comforts. It was customary then for men to stay bachelors until late in life. Saturday night was when you would see the "ploughies" in town. They enjoyed their weekly dose of contact with society and its liquid pleasures.

Hometown

A major bonus to the town was the Royal Naval Air Station Condor, a training base for the Fleet Air Arm. This provided a steady influx of trainees and a means for the town's younger females to widen their horizons. Many local girls did marry those young trainees and left to see the world. For me it was a brief, if somewhat glamorous look at military life. I loved to cycle out to the base and watch the Sea Furies and Sea Tempests practicing deck landings.

Never comfortable on or in water, regardless of depth, the Navy was not my calling. However it made me aware that if ever I wanted to become part of such an organization, I had better make an effort to prepare myself. This was easier said than done. I was and continue to be one of life's perpetual under achievers. Interested only in soccer and flying, I found school a chore. I wasn’t really good at anything apart from soccer but I had little trouble in gaining pass marks in all subjects except French and Music. Having never heard of a French musician achieving hero status as a soccer player or as a flying ace, my apparent shortcomings didn't trouble me.

Primary schools were all neighborhood schools and catered for those living near to the schools location. You attended from the age of five until you were twelve years old. Ladyloan was a “fisher” school as it was located opposite the sea front. Inverbrothock was situated close to the Brothock Burn on the edge of town where newer housing was being built. Abbey as the name implies, was situated adjacent to Arbroath Abbey. There was one Parochial school, St Thomas, a Roman Catholic School. Keptie primary school was close to Arbroath High School at the West end of town. The High School was the only school in town where primary, secondary and further education was a continuous process. Mainly children, whose parents lived in the posh West End, attended the High School. The other primary school was Parkhouse. Although the name sounds quite grand and upscale, this was no clone of an English prep school. It was referred to as the “Ragged Academy,” my first school!

The town was brought sharply into the national spotlight in 1952. The "Stone of Destiny," was stolen from under the

Coronation Chair in Westminster Abbey, London. It was "found" in Arbroath Abbey. The Abbey with its long history seemed a more fitting home for the relic than Westminster. One of my High School teachers was involved in the "finding" of the Stone. I would have been more impressed if he had injected as much enthusiasm and daring into his teaching as he did into his politics.

A Clydesdale standing in front of a blacksmiths shop was a sure sign that sparks were about to fly. New shoes! The big man in his leather apron would beat a shoe out of a piece of red-hot glowing iron. He made it look so easy, as real masters of any craft do. Lifting each big shaggy hoof in turn he would pry off the horse's old shoe then prepare the hoof with a rough file and a paring knife. I always cringed at that bit it looked so barbaric and painful though the horse rarely flinched. Grabbing the cherry red shoe from the coals with a large pair of tongs he would sear the shoe onto the hoof producing an acrid and unpleasant smell. A large cloud of steam followed as the shoe was plunged into a barrel of cold water. The holes were then spiked on the anvil. A hammer and nails would finish the job. Wherever I walk on cobbled streets I think of horses and the blacksmith.

Coal, milk and green groceries, were delivered by horse drawn carts. Running behind these carts, our little gang would jump and hang on to the back board, swinging our legs off the ground and over the axle as the horse plodded along. Of course after months of this foolishness the inevitable happened. Ally Connor, mistimed his jump and his leg was caught in the wheel. None of us had the courage to stop and assist. We ran, leaving Ally to his fate. He had to have half his leg amputated!

Months later, upon his return he let us all look and touch what we had been unwilling to view at the time. Once our morbid curiosity had been satisfied, he hid the stump from view with a specially knitted sock. To his great credit he refused to let this tragedy hold him back. He played football with us just as he did before. His crutch provided both a support and an effective tripping tool. I've always had a quiet admiration for Ally. Life has not treated him kindly.

Thick hessian sacks filled with lumps of coal, being carried on a flat cart, meant that the coalman was coming. Unlike the blacksmith, the coal man's center of gravity was closer to the ground. His badge of office was a heavy, leather waistcoat, adorned with shiny metal studs. Carrying each bag on his back he dumped the contents, amid a cloud of black dust, into the coal cellar. Always subject to scrutiny by the lady of the house who expected full value for her money, he was frequently chastised for having put in “ower much dross.” (Small pieces and dust)

Tam Robb was our coal man. He had a specific route for each day of the week and the horse knew the routes as well as he did. The horse started and stopped with commands that I have no words for. A rough clicking sound spat out of the side of the coalman’s mouth. I swear, if he delivered the wrong number of bags the horse wouldn’t move until he got it right! On Saturday mornings I would sometimes get to ride up on the cart. I would crack the reins just the way they did in the movies. There was no question about who was the boss. That horse had no idea what “giddy up” meant.

Local Knowledge

The town had two newspapers, The Guide and The Herald, one published on Friday and the other on Saturday. Both contained local news only. The daily paper was The Dundee Courier and Advertiser, what a mouthful! Most other people thought so to and it was always just called "The Courier." The evening paper was 'The Evening Telegraph," known locally as "The Tilly." Both the daily and the evening papers had part of a column on the back page, which was printed in red ink. The "Stop Press," the latest and hottest news, in abbreviated form.

Shopping was pretty much confined to two areas, the High Street and the West Port. I think every town in Britain had a High Street! The West Port was named as such because it ran from East to West, from the harbor to the railway station. Daily shopping was a way of life and when I say shopping I mean for food. After the war there were no such things as refrigerators or freezers. In the winter months you would put milk or butter outside on the window ledge to help keep it fresh but normally you shopped on a daily basis. Most shops were only open for five and a half days a week, from 9am to 6pm and almost all closed for one hour at noon. Wednesday was a half-holiday, all shops closed at noon. On Sunday there were no shops open.

The long shadow of John Knox still darkened most of Scotland and thoughts of pleasure and penance were constantly at odds. The "drink" was the demon in most working class homes. Sunday and Church were synonymous. Scotland was primarily divided into two religions, Protestant and Catholic. Every large city had two football teams, one Catholic and the other Protestant, the most notorious being Glasgow, where Celtic and Rangers were the ecclesiastical standard bearers.

For as many places of worship, there was more than double that number of public houses. Many pubs had what they called a "Snug" or a "Private" which allowed men or women to enter into a very small sheltered area for service. Children were often sent to one of these to have the family flagon filled with draft beer or stout. The nearest such establishment to me, was Barnett's. I often wondered what they did behind the polished glass and wood swing doors that caused so much noise and laughter. Saturday night was the busiest of the week with the influx of farm workers and naval trainees. My interest in pubs has not waned to this very day

Cigarettes and tobacco were only sold in Newsagent's & Tobacconists shops. As Mother and Gran both smoked, I knew where the newsagent's were from an early age. There were many different brands and strengths of cigarettes from which to choose. Woodbines came in small envelopes containing as few as five cigarettes, all the way up to a pack containing twenty. The navy seemed to be predominantly displayed in the advertising of tobacco. Sailors and ships adorned many different brands. However as an incentive to the undecided or those with little inclination for the sea, cigarette cards were offered as an inducement to purchase. Cigarette cards became very valuable commodities; ranking right up there with hens rings and marbles.

Not every manufacturer put cards in their packets. Some were in color, some portrayed soccer players or racehorses. Others actually had individual flowers depicted on them; get an education as you puffed your life away! The best in my humble opinion were the soccer cards that came in cigarettes with the brand name "Turf." Now I didn't care if the product tasted like its name I wanted the cards. Mum and Gran didn't seem to notice.

Chewing tobacco and pipe tobacco were still very popular and a number of the older fisher women smoked small white clay pipes. The pipes weren't packed in individual wrappers or boxes they came in a cardboard "flat." Being fragile many would be broken or chipped. We used to get the chipped ones for a farthing. Great for blowing bubbles or for pretending you were a real smoker. The newsagent's shop sold another item that was more easily broken. It was an essential to the wellbeing of any household, the gas mantle!

This device balanced precariously on three minute ceramic points over the end of the gas pipe above your mantle-piece. It allowed gas to be trapped and burned within its fragile gossamer like envelope. This was the only means of illumination in the house apart from the glow from an open fireplace or a candle. Many a night I was sent out to find a gas mantle. They cost three pence each and came in a thin, square cardboard box. You always had to check inside the box before you left the shop to be sure the mantle wasn't damaged. Once you left the shop no return was possible. The frustration of getting all the way home and finding a damaged mantle inside the box was worse than dropping it as you hurried up the stairs. There was no excuse either way it was another three pence and a further strain on limited finances.

The town's streets were illuminated, a generous description, by gas lamps. The lamps were lit every night and extinguished every morning. The "leerie," pedaled his bicycle, with his special pole over his shoulder and did the rounds regardless of the weather. On winter nights under the "lampy" was always a good meeting place for friends or for those of a more romantic persuasion. We had a "lampy' above the entrance to our front door which was called a "pend." This was a wide tunnel guarded by a large wooden door built to allow access for a horse and cart into a sheltered area under the dwellings above. Young lovers often would sneak inside the "pend" for privacy. Knowing a couple to be in there, we would climb over the wall and enter from the back. Then it was a question of making scary noises or staying quiet and watching. The lack of a formal sex education often made the latter the most enjoyable course.

By 1950 the exporting of herring and sailcloth had gone the way of the sailing ships. This was the age of steam and engines of the day were massive coal burners with individual names. "The Flying Scotsman" held the worlds speed record for a number of years and plied its trade running from

England to Scotland. Kerr's miniature railway couldn't afford the real thing but used the name anyway. Train spotting was popular but I wasn't interested. I wanted to ride in the trains not take down their numbers. Train stations were noisy, dirty places covered in coal dust and smoke. Stations waiting rooms had polished linoleum floors and constantly burning coal fires. This was a feature that I would come to fully appreciate much later during my service life.

No description of the town would be complete without mentioning the places of entertainment. The town boasted only one set of traffic lights but we had three cinemas! No other form of entertainment that I knew of charged a shilling and transported you into another dimension! The Palace, The Picture House and The Olympia were purveyors of escapism, providing widows on worlds that were beyond my imaginings. I would eagerly await the arrival of the new billposters. The "poster mannie" with his roll of bills and his bucket of glue, would slap his brush and position the folded sheets all in one seamless motion. Posters were blue or red lettering on a white background, the week's fare of "pictures" without pictures.

Dancing was a popular pastime and was catered for by a number of dance halls. The Templars and a number of cafes had dance floors but the Marine

Ballroom was the biggest and the best. Dancing was taught at school, the waltz, foxtrot and quickstep. Dancing with a teenager of the same sex held little interest for me. It didn't quite capture the spirit or the steps necessary to make you a desirable partner on a Saturday night.

The town boasted an Olympic size swimming pool, open air! Who ever thought that one up never visited the East Coast of Scotland in the summer! The indoor swimming pool and baths were located at Marketgate. I used the baths regularly as we had no running hot water at home. One of the main attractions for me was the Brylcream machine. The Royal Air Force was always referred to as "Brylcream Boys." They were my boyhood heroes; any association no matter how tenuous was worth pursuing. For the princely sum of a penny, I would put my hand under the spigot push in the slide and voila. A dollop of the famous, thick, white hairdressing would plop into the palm of my hand. If monetarily challenged it was possible to put your mouth around the spigot and suck out a portion for free. Of course, I would never have stooped so low! No pun intended.

Founded in 1178 by King William the Lion, Arbroath Abbey is famous in Scottish history for its association with the Declaration of Arbroath, in which Scotland's nobles swore their independence from England. Some details of this declaration can be found in the Constitution of the United States of America.

As a seaside town the structures of greatest importance to the town's inhabitants were of a nautical nature, primarily the Signal Tower which overlooks the harbor and is partly responsible for the town's Scottish name, the "Red Lichties. The other structure of consequence is the Bellrock lighthouse some eleven miles off shore to which day trips were offered.

National attention was focused on the town by the theft of a fishing boat by a schoolboy! A four day international search of the North Sea found the missing boat adrift in the

middle of a storm. The schoolboy, tired and hungry was towed back to port

A more tragic event known locally as Black Tuesday occurred. In turbulent sea's the lifeboat returning from a false alarm failed to negotiate the tricky harbor entrance and capsized. Six of the seven man crew was drowned.

Entertainment

The major entertainment of the nineteen forties and fifties was the "pictures." Cinemas were open 7 days a week, with no matinee on Sunday. They were large imposing buildings sporting bright multi-colored neon sign's. The only neon signs in town. They had indoor plumbing and carpets like nothing I had ever seen before. From the age of six I started going to the "pictures" and I loved them.

The high, decorative ceilings adorned with huge chandeliers made me feel that I was in a palace of sorts. Lighting that responded to the touch of a switch and huge red colored curtains that opened and closed at the whim of an unseen hand. The opening of those huge curtains heralded the start of the evening's fare. All conversation ceased the lights dimmed, the sound and vision washing over the expectant audience. During evening shows this vision was viewed through a blue haze as the smokers lit up.

With three cinemas in town there was always something playing that was of interest. You would get an A or a B movie along with a couple of shorts, a serial episode, a cartoon, the news and trailers for the coming week. The Palace, aptly named, was the most luxurious of the three cinemas. It was also the furthest from my home in Millgate Loan. It was impossible to walk to the pictures without passing a chip shop or a sweetie shop. Now this may sound like a good thing. If I only had enough money for the cheapest seats the smells and thoughts of the fare provided by these places, was torture. “One day,” I promised myself, “One day, I’ll go to the pictures any time I want and buy as many sweeties as I can eat,” ah such simple pleasures.

The Olympia was affectionately known as the “flech hoose.” This wasn’t really true it had no more fleas than any of the other cinemas but it was the oldest of the three. You had to climb a number of outside stairs to enter the foyer. Huddling against the wind and rain, perched on seemingly vertical steps, was not a good start to the evening. However it made up for these shortcomings by showing serials three times a week. These ranged from the ancient “Perils of Pauline” to a more modern “Captain Marvel.”

In a pre-microchip age special effects were primitive. Captain Marvel turned into a cartoon character when he flew out of the window or performed some other impossible feat. I didn’t care it was all in the mind anyway. What did get to be upsetting was when you were left hanging. A situation that seemed impossible at the end of one episode showed a slightly different ending in the next episode allowing our hero to escape. This was commonly known as "swicking." But if you really wanted to believe, it didn't matter.

I sat through serials of "Zorro," "Last of the Mohicans," "Flash Gordon," "Superman," "Batman and Robin" and God knows how many others. Edgar Kennedy was always a klutz, the Three Stooges were always funny, and Oliver and Hardy were always being stupid. I mustn't forget the cowboys, Roy Rogers, Gene Autry and The Lone Ranger and Tonto. William Boyd was the silver haired "Hopalong Cassidy" and the only cowboy who dressed in black. No wonder I have a head full of rubbish after watching years of that.

The Picture House was more modern than the Olympia but not as opulent as the Palace. Located on the High Street it was close to the Olympia, which on occasion caused indecision when both were showing pictures that I wanted to see.

Each of the movie houses belonged to a particular distribution network although I wasn't aware of that at the time. It meant that only one cinema could show a particular film. Long lines always indicated the popular pictures.

Cinemas used to have posters and display cases outside showing what was currently playing and what was coming in the next few days or weeks. The display cases showed photographs of scenes from the picture, “show casing” the stars. The photographs were black and white of course just like the pictures. Three days was the normal showing cycle of a picture. The popular pictures played on Friday’s, Saturday’s and Sunday.

Saturday night was not a night to go to the pictures if you could only afford the cheap seats. Lines of people waiting to get in meant you had little chance of getting a ticket. They had an usher come down the line shouting, to let you know when seats became available. “Two singles up front” or “A double in the balcony”

Seating was divided into sections from the front working backwards. Prices increased the further back you went. The balcony was for big spenders and courting couples. A constant picture goer I had a stiff neck from looking up at the movie from the first row, half the time I was close enough to the screen to be in the picture!

Entering the darkened theatre you presented your ticket stub to the usherette she would shine her flashlight on the floor so as not to disturb the patrons as she guided you to your seat. It was possible if the place wasn’t full, to switch to a more expensive seat. Getting caught however meant being ejected. I never could relax when I did that and would shrink down in my stolen seat every time she passed. I do remember there being an organist at the Palace and the Olympia for a short while. Playing during the intermission, the words of the song were put up on the screen for you to sing along. No wonder I remember the words to songs that are from an earlier generation.

The managers of these palaces of make believe were of high standing in the community. Dressed in black dinner jackets and bow ties, they looked like refugees from a cancelled dinner party. They stood in the foyer observing and greeting customers as they came in. As frequently as I attended the pictures, to be acknowledged was so far above me as to be unthinkable. I had no inkling as to where these men lived or what they wore when they weren't on duty. They could have been wheeled out, dusted and switched "On" prior to each performance for all I knew. How grand it would have been to brag that your father, brother or uncle actually managed one of these picture houses. It would have ruined the image though; Gods don't have names like Bill, Fred or Dad.

There were a few memorable pictures. Boris Karloff as "Frankenstein" and Bela Lugosi as "Dracula" both made an impact. However the movie that probably had the biggest effect on me was "The Wizard of Oz," the first of the epic movies. This was the first film I ever saw that was in color although it started in black and white and I thought I had been "swicked." The Lion needed courage, the Tin Man needed a heart and the Scarecrow needed a brain, things that we all need in life. Having a yellow brick road to follow wouldn't hurt either. Most pictures had a moral. Good guys always won and bad guys always lost. The good guys wore white and bad guys wore black

The Palace came up with a novel idea for a Saturday morning matinee. You had to be a member to get in. It was called the ABC Minors. This was bedlam on a large scale! Letting one hundred and fifty kids aged between six and fifteen loose inside a darkened building, is asking for trouble. There were two adult ushers who walked around trying to instill law and order. Monitors were appointed as assistants to the ushers, to look after specific rows of seats. Naturally the kids that got these positions were the biggest kids it was like letting the inmates run the asylum.

It was great fun! You got a singsong before the pictures started. You got to throw stuff at the kids a few rows in front when the local make belief cowboys Rex and Tex were being stupid. When the lights went out and the picture started, you got to cheer for the good guy and boo the bad guy. I loved it. The smartest thing management ever did was keeping the balcony closed. When it was over it was only noon. You had the rest of the day left to go and do something else.

Apart from the pictures, there was Gayfield on a Saturday afternoon, the home of AFC, the "Red Lichties." Normally the schedule was one Saturday at home and the next Saturday away. I worked Saturday afternoons and when the team was at home it was torture for me. The roar of the crowd told me when the home team had scored but I never knew who was winning. Laying my message bike against the wall and standing on the seat, I could glimpse some of the action. Arbroath FC still holds the record for the highest number of goals scored in a professional football match, 36 to nil! The Aberdeen Bon Accord, their opponents, if that word is truly applicable, is no longer in existence.

Summer entertainment was eclectic it included anything from sheepdog trials to swimming and from paddling to putting. With the soccer season over Gayfield was a place with seating available for outdoor activities. The most unique event held there were the sheepdog trials. I found it fascinating. Watching man and dog outwitting a bunch of unwilling and skittish sheep was akin to witnessing ESP. Shepherds were in great demand especially from the part of the Empire commonly referred to as "down under." The Empire had long gone but the name was still loosely used to describe the new Commonwealth.

The outdoor swimming pool was open for those with a head for heights or Olympic ambitions. Fifty yards further away a large paddling pool sufficed for those of us with lesser goals. The penny arcade directly opposite the paddling pool was only open during the summer months. Further along the sea front a collection of chutes, swings and roundabouts straddled a small white building. This teahouse had a shop in front and public conveniences at the rear.

This was the last "pit stop" en route to the pony rides and Kerr's miniature railway. You could continue on and picnic at the aptly named "White Elephant," a Victorian structure that never seemed to have any obvious function. A string of large concrete blocks, built and placed ostensibly to repel German armor, ran all the way to Elliot. They were the most expensive windbreaks in town, providing privacy for "sun worshipers" and courting couples alike. If you were too tired to walk back into town, you could catch a real train at Elliot Junction.

My favorite summer pastime was putting. The putting greens at the low common were beautifully kept. Grass was mowed with great care to enhance the subtleties of the grain. Diabolically difficult hole placements meant afternoons of concentration and competition. The problem was that you had to pay for

every round you played! This may have seemed fair to the holidaymakers but I felt that regular, skilled players deserved fairer treatment. If you planned it just right, you could sneak in extra rounds for free. Waiting until the man that gave out the balls and clubs was busy with other people, you snuck back to the first hole. You had to be careful though when returning your club and ball, the old guy collecting the money had a pretty good memory. Wait for a crowd at the kiosk then slip your club and ball back into the selection on the counter. Willie, my cousin Percy and I played for the British Open, the US Open, the PGA and the Masters all in one afternoon then did it all over again the very next day.

There were tennis courts for the more athletic minded and of course any number of beaches on which to sun bathe on. The water temperature restricted bathing to the hardy and the foolhardy. You could take a trip to the cliffs in a "Pleasure Boat" and sail through the caves. Gannet's, shags and colorful puffins perched noisily for your viewing pleasure. Fishing was another favorite activity. A rod cast from the harbor entrance, or a small rented boat with lines.

For three weeks in the summer the travelling fairground, the "switchie" came to town. This was a great place to meet girls but you had to have money. Holiday girls hung out there looking for boys to treat them. You always went dressed up to the "switchie," you never knew, you just might get a "click!" Popular music blared out. Kay Starr singing "Wheel of Fortune" comes to mind. The "Chair O Planes" the "Waltzers" and the "Dodgem Cars" were the top draws.

Bertram's Circus was another two or three week visitor in the summer. I never was very fond of the circus. As I lived on the main road going south to the public common, everything coming into town went past my front door. Strange noises in the street were the tip-off that the circus was in town. It was always early morning when it arrived so avoiding blocking the narrow main road. Looking out the attic window I would see all the brightly painted circus caravans, trucks and exotic animals like elephants and llamas parading outside. It was a special show, put on just for me or so I believed. Dressing quickly I would rush down the stairs. Still rubbing the sleep from my eyes and with my brother on my heels I followed the caravan. Like a modern "Pied Piper" the colorful parade collected more and more kids with every street it passed. We would all gather at the low common to watch the raising of the "big top."

Radio was the year round entertainment. It was a big clunky veneered box, which was not at all portable. The first thing you needed was a wet accumulator. And the second thing you needed was a wet accumulator. Commonly referred to as "qummies," these provided the power to run the set. Why would you need two you might ask? Murphy's Law was alive and well. If you only had one "qummie" you could bet that it would fail just when you were listening

to your favorite program. Two therefore was the minimum number. Now having two “qummies” didn't help much either unless they were charged. I knew my way to Black the electrician's where the process of top up and trickle charging was revealed to me.

Radio allowed me to listen to the announcement of the end of WWII, Bruce Woodcock fighting Joe Baksi and Jimmy Cowan's Wembley. For me radio died after 1953 as TV became affordable. But what a year to finish on, the present Queen's Coronation, Gordon Richards won the Derby and Stanley Matthew's won a Cup Final medal. Hilary and Tensing conquered Everest!

Gracie Fields went on forever with “The Biggest Aspidistra in the World” and George Formby was still “Standing on the Corner.” Billy Cotton woke us up on Sunday mornings with his “Wakey, Wakey” cry.

Wilfred Pickles always had new talent to present and

money to give away for "having a go." Lunchtime was never complete without the evergreen, "Workers Playtime." Leslie Welch, "The Memory Man," never failed.

Radio provided all our music, mostly big bands with name singers. It also provided the first "pop" songs for a country starved of entertainment. Jo Stafford, Guy Mitchell, Rosemary Clooney, Doris Day, Al Martino and Perry Como, became household names in Britain. Radio Luxemburg was the broadcaster of most of this type of music. Tastes would change again in the early fifties when a swivel hipped young Cajun called Elvis, exploded on the scene. Who knew fifty years on he still wouldn't have left the building.

The old style cafes were changing into coffee bars with jukeboxes. The High Street was still the best place to meet and greet people. A new generation was fueling the economy, WWII was history that most wanted to forget. Record players were the rage. It was a period of mixed attitudes likes and dislikes. The free Punch and Judy shows held out at the low common became less and less popular. Cycling was in decline as cars and better roads started to appear.

My Family

I was delivered at home in Park Street, March 25th, 1938. My father went to war in 1939. When he came back I was almost eight years old. He was part of the British Expeditionary Force (BEF) that was sent to help France. Along with thousands of others, he was captured on the beach at St Valery. Unlike Dunkirk there was no flotilla of small ships for these men. He spent six long years as a POW. He never talked about or told me about his wartime experiences. How bitter he must have felt at having to give up those precious years I can only imagine.

L/SERGEANT HAMILTON WILSON

Intimation has been received by Mrs Wilson, 7 Millgate Loan, Arbroath, that her husband, L/Sergeant Hamilton Wilson, Royal Artillery, is missing.

L/Sgt. Hamilton Wilson.

L/Sergeant Wilson, who is 30, was a Territorial, and was called up when war was declared. He is chauffeur to an Army official, and went to France in January after a short leave.

L/Sergeant Wilson was formerly employed as a van driver with Goldberg's (Warehouse) Ltd. in Glasgow. He has a family of two boys.

My mother was the only child of my Granny Ogg. Although christened Euphemia, I never, ever heard any one call my mother by any other name than Effie. Not a real surprise eh? Gran and Mum were the mainstays of family life for my younger brother Willie and me. Although we were 16 months apart, we were often taken for twins. It was a standing joke in the family in later years about my reply when asked by doting women, “Are you twins?” My reply was always a sincere, “No we’re brothers.” The reply was accompanied with a questioning look and a thought that people must be dumb not to see that. Unknown to me a man who asked me this question at the salvage dump was a reporter. I gave him my standard answer and it appeared in print in the Sunday Post!

During my growing up, Mum enjoyed a certain celebrity, at least in her mind. Always a stylish dresser and conscious of her appearance, she drummed her values and her sayings into my brother and I. “Manners and clothes maketh the man,” she would say. I was confused we were boys not men and who did we know that we could use manners on? In later years the ability to appear presentable and be polite stood me in good stead. Her advice instilled more than a modicum of confidence in both her sons.

Apart from a short stay in Glasgow, where she was a professional dancer at the Locarno Ballroom, mother had lived all her life close to her mother, my Granny Ogg. She had not been without ambition or talent but it seemed that for some reason, mother was destined to be a small town girl. After marrying my father in Glasgow she and her new husband returned to Arbroath. Married 3 years prior to WWII she had two children before seeing her husband leave for war. Waiting six long years for his return from a variety of German POW camps couldn’t have been easy.

Thumbing through the family photo album I am struck by how Mum posed. Posed, that was the word. It showed in every picture, awareness of the camera, never a casual or unflattering angle. No half shut eyes or funny face. This was emphasized even more when I turned to the page that displayed the only letter that she had ever kept, a letter inviting her to Dundee for a film screen test. I presumed that the screen test hadn't gone as well as she had expected, otherwise I would probably have been born in California not Scotland. What a disappointment life must have been for her but she always put on a cheerful front. She constantly expected "something to turn up" and was resourceful in the extreme. Granny Ogg was ever present in my young life. She was a surrogate who lived either next door or across the street. Purporting to be a smoker she never inhaled. Honest! I think it gave her something to do or maybe it was just to keep her hands busy. Strange, there are no photos in the family album of her with a cigarette.

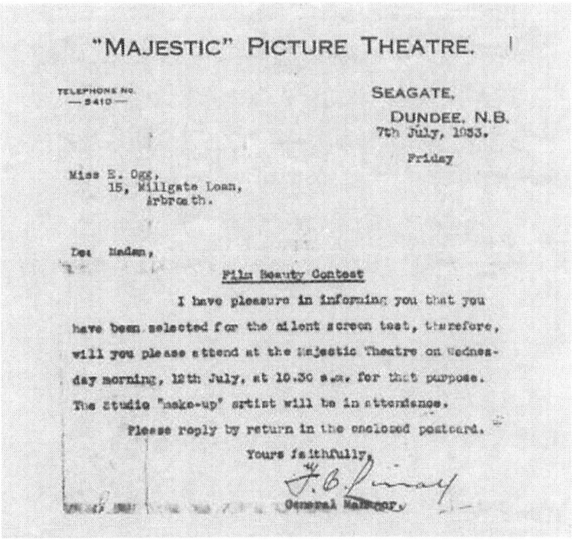

"MAJESTIC" PICTURE THEATRE.

TELEPHONE NO.
—5410—

SEAGATE,
DUNDEE, N.B.
7th July, 1933.

Friday

Miss E. Ogg,
15, Millgate Loan,
Arbroath.

Dear Madam,

Film Beauty Contest

I have pleasure in informing you that you have been selected for the silent screen test, therefore, will you please attend at the Majestic Theatre on Wednesday morning, 12th July, at 10.30 a.m. for that purpose. The Studio "make-up" artist will be in attendance.

Please reply by return in the enclosed postcard.

Yours faithfully,

J. B. [illegible]

General Manager.

Gran was very proud of my brother and me showing us off at every opportunity. In later life she had to resort to wearing a hearing aid and this upset her vanity greatly. Often she would hide it under her cardigan, leaving it switched off or just “forgetting” and leaving it at home altogether. She enjoyed her walk-about every morning, picking up the bits and pieces she needed. More importantly she met people she knew and enjoyed having a “crack.”

My brother and I worried about her being on her own when we moved and tried to give her things that would make her life more comfortable. To help prevent her from having to carry coal upstairs Willie and I bought her an electric fire. Carrying buckets of coal upstairs may have been good exercise but one slip on those concrete steps! She never did get used to “that new-fangled thing” and went back to her old ways, saying that it was too expensive. Resigned to that, our next attempt at helping was buying her a gas poker. It was something she could use without having to practice the black art of lighting a coal fire with paper “sticks.” So much for that idea, “too much trouble” she said. We bought her a transistor radio when they first came out but she didn’t use it either. She had outlived all her friends and she was tired. “I wish I wis awa,” she would often say. She lived to see both my brother and I married. Gran left many happy memories to go along with the number of pennies that she slipped Willie and me.

The innumerable cups of tea and biscuits that she provided along with her cheery outlook are not forgotten.

Gran Ogg had three brothers, Lawson, Chris and Ted, as well as two sisters, Nellie and Mary. Ted became a golf professional and when last heard of was working in Bergen, Norway. Never quite figured that one out! Chris lived in Perth and I only met him the once. He looked very much like Prime Minister Chamberlain. Thin with a clipped moustache and looking very uncomfortable in his stiff white detachable shirt collar. Both Lawson and Nellie lived in the town. Neither was more than a 10-minute walk from where I lived in Millgate Loan. I would see both of them quite regularly although I never felt that close to either. Compared to Aunt Mary they seemed staid and old, not much fun. Mary lived in Yonkers, New York. I had never met her until Willie's wedding. During the war she used to send Mum a parcel twice a year. They were awesome as far as my brother and I was concerned. Jeans, sneakers, candy, chewing gum and comics!

During the period when my father was a POW, Uncle Lawson tried to be a father figure but it never quite worked. We had become independent as a family and didn't take kindly to being told what to do. That doesn't mean that we lacked respect it was just that times had changed. After the death of his first wife Eva, Lawson had remarried. His second wife, Violet, had two boys of her own, David and Boyd. Mum always took us to Uncle Lawson's to "first foot." We had many a New Year drink at his house. Violet, in her lovely voice, would sing her party piece, "The Rose of Trallee."

Uncle Lawson had one son from his first marriage, Lawson Jr. He in turn had two daughters, Betty and Frances as well as a son, Lawson. There was a falling out between my Uncle Lawson and his son and they stopped talking to each other. Years went by. Father and son both passed away without ever speaking to each other again! I've always wondered what could have been so bad as to cause such an action. Life is way too short for that.

Aunt Nellie lived at Gowan Street, which was close to the railway station. She had two daughters, Mary and Helen. Helen had a son, Percy and a daughter, Dorothy. Mary never married. Percy lived with his Gran and Mary. Percy and I are three years apart and have kept our friendship alive to this day.

I never met or knew of a grandfather on either side of my family. There is probably a story or two in that sentence, but it is unknown to me. My paternal grandmother, Granny Wilson lived in Greenock, which is on the West Coast of Scotland near Glasgow. That is where my father was born and brought up. As a young boy I remember meeting members of my father's family in Greenock. My father's sister Annie was a very nice person and always treated my brother and me very well. Granny Wilson's house was quiet, clean and "posh" compared to how we lived. She was a kind lady who seemed quite lost in knowing what to do on the rare occasion when my brother and I visited her.

Money and Status

Health, wealth and happiness may have been the toast in the pubs but it certainly didn't materialize outside. Good health was largely dependent on the food that you ate. Rationing dictated that unless you could find a supplement. There was little oral hygiene and a trip to the dentist was something to be very afraid of. Doctors did visit but only for serious conditions. Outbreaks of chicken pox, measles, scarlet fever and ringworm were allowed to run their course.

As a youngster of eight, I had no concept of what wealth meant in monetary terms. To me a hundred pounds was a king's ransom. This was a time when grown men earned shillings a week for six days work! Happiness was tied to a wage coming into the home.

For many families where fathers or brothers had returned from the war, happiness was a long time in coming. Having survived the war some men wouldn't or couldn't work. They drank too much, fought too much and in some cases simply just wandered away.

As is invariably the case when people are all on the same level and share the same conditions, no thought is given to status in life. We were all poor. No matter which pal's house I went to it was the same. There was little to eat, sparse furniture and money only for the necessities of life, milk, bread, potatoes and porridge. Toast and oatmeal are still staples in my diet. Many homes had the table permanently set or laid out. Not formal settings you understand. The condiments, brown sauce, butter, sugar bowl and teapot all graced a colorful waxed tablecloth, which never saw the washing green. Tables, set ready and waiting for a dreamed of feast which never appeared.

Every family that I knew paid rent had an insurance man and a "packy man." The "packy man" was someone who came round to your door and sold you things like socks, underwear and such like. The one's I remember were Indian. They traveled between Dundee and Arbroath lugging their battered suitcases from door to door.

You put so much down and paid so much a week. No collateral was needed. With nowhere to go and no way to get there, he was pretty sure of getting his weekly payment. "HP" (Hire Purchase) is known today as credit. It was extended by legitimate business's to allow you to buy "luxury" goods. This included items such as radios, record players and much later, TV's and washing machines. To qualify for the "Drip" as it was more commonly called, took little more than presenting a pay stub and being able to mist up a mirror with your breath.

Friday was not a good day to be around the house. It was payday, if anyone was working that is. All the collectors of money showed up on Friday. If you didn't have money to pay them you had to be inventive. As I think back on it, those guys' must have heard every excuse in the book and then some. Payment was probably rendered in other ways apart from money. Purely conjecture on my part of course but tainted by life experience. Dad may have spent an hour or two at the pub before coming home or stopped at the bookies to pay off his "line." When his "bunnet" was thrown down the lobby, I knew there was no money coming home that day.

There were investments of a kind that most families would put money into. The easiest and most dependable one was an insurance policy but rarely did a policy run its full term. It was invariably cashed in and generally was used as a "bankie." There were stamps that you could buy at the Post Office, which you stuck into a special book provided for the purpose. The stamps could be cashed in at any time for the full face value. Then there was Vernon's or Littlewoods, the pools. They provided a sheet of soccer fixtures on which you selected your picks for away wins, home wins, draws and a hundred other permutations. Win the “eight results” and you could retire for life on seventy five thousand pounds!

I must mention one other monetary requirement and that was the need to keep money for the “meter.” The gas meter that is. All houses had their own meter. No money, no gas, no light and no hot food. The local Gas Board provided the gas meter. It was a heavy metal box with a slot into which you inserted coins of a certain denomination. You then turned a small handle allowing the coin to drop and the gas to flow. It had a gauge showing how much longer the gas would last without inserting any more coins. My first memory of a meter is of one that accepted pennies, big brown “coppers.” The “meter money” was stashed in a secret place within each household and was often used as the bank of last resort.

The “meter mannie” was responsible for emptying the meter and working out any over payment. There was always cash back, as the meter was set to over charge! Imagine that today. Naturally the “gasman” was always welcome. He would remove the coin box from the meter with a special key. Sitting at the table he would carefully count the contents. A paper receipt along with the overcharge was put to one side. This was always welcome money. On occasion, in desperation, meters were broken into, an offence that merited jail time.

On the other side of investments there was betting. There was horse racing, dog racing, pigeon racing, darts, dice, dominos and cards. Probably there were a host of other games of chance that I have never heard of as well. Most could be conducted within the confines of a pub. What is wrong with that picture?

I did say we were all in the same boat but that was not strictly true. Men "in business" had their homes well away from the rest of us, only showing up in the morning to open up shop. I do not recall any of these business men, having a car.

They did send their children to schools other than the ones that we went to. I never thought about that then. There were rich men in the town, most resided in the West End. Where their wealth came from I can only guess but most likely mill owners, engineers, merchants and landlords. Many had made money in India in the textile trade. When I started delivering groceries I discovered the West End.

To be elected as Town Provost some degree of affluence or business acumen was required. As in most small towns mainly a clique of prominent people held the office of Town Provost. Town Provosts when in office had two gas lamps posted outside their residence. The Arbroath town crest was painted on one glass pane of each lamp. These lamps were lit and extinguished daily by the town lamp lighter. When any Provost retired from office, one lamppost was removed. The other remained in place as a sign of respect and recognition for public service. The portcullis, as displayed on the Arbroath town crest, was depicted on the rear of the old brass colored "thrupenny bit" and the copper colored farthing.

Schools

Just kidding, it really wasn't this bad but close! I attended primary school from the age of five until the age of twelve. When I was thirteen I attended the High school for my secondary education. I finished school at the grand old age of fifteen. Up until 1945 the school leaving age was fourteen! Most of the primary school's had been built in the late 1800's and looked like they had been modeled on Victorian workhouses, dark and unwelcoming. Iron railings surrounded schoolyards acting as physical barriers of detention and division. A number of these railings had been cut down to provide war material. Apart from leaving dangerous metal stumps behind, their intended function was not missed.

Each school had a janitor. His duties called for ringing the morning and afternoon bell for starting class and the bell that ended playtimes. He also acted as referee, policeman and father figure. A fifteen-minute grace period was allowed after the start of class before the janitor padlocked the schoolyard gate. If you were late you were punished and if you were very late you were locked out. Being small and thin I could slide through the railings for clandestine trips to Peggy's for a sherbet dip, a stick of cinnamon or if flush, a hot meat pie.

At break time the schoolyard teemed with children of all ages and sizes. Although the classes were coed, metal railings separated the boys and girls in the schoolyard. Falling foul of one of the bigger kids was something to be avoided at all costs. Playground fights were common. Fighting was punished with a taste the "belt" and was meted out by the "Heed." As a deterrent it was normally meted out in front of whatever class he happened to be teaching at the time. I enjoyed watching the bullies getting whacked with that thick leather strap. It worked for some of them but others had a harder life at home and the threat of the "belt" was no deterrent. Few of them cried and even fewer changed their behavior. On school property, teachers had full authority and sparing the rod was rarely practiced.

Every morning at 8.30 we gathered for the Morning Prayer before being split up for our classes. There were no books! We each had our own slate, which you brought to school with you and a stone pencil that you wrote with. I have no idea what the proper name for it was but it was always referred to as "skiley." The slate, on which you wrote, was a common or garden roofing slate. The only difference was that it had a wooden frame around it. If you were unlucky enough to drop your slate on its corner, it was history.

Lessons were based on the "three R's." This phrase never, ever, made sense to me. Reading, I'll go along with that. Writing, come on. Last but not least, Arithmetic. No matter, the "three R's" have stood me in good stead all my life. Classroom mornings began by reciting the "times" tables from one through ten by rote. Boring, like a parrot. I rarely paid attention until one morning, whack! A wrap on the knuckles with the edge of a ruler brought tears to my eyes. Lesson learned, pay attention, keep a low profile and keep your hands under your desk.

Every day I had to recite the alphabet and then do one hour of what is now called "cursive writing." I don't remember what we called it, "real writing' I think. Struggling to form those intricate characters and curves on the very faint lines scribed on my slate was a challenge. My first teacher, Miss Duncan not only taught me to write but also became my first crush. I thought she was an angel sent from heaven, flawless. All my teachers for the three years which I attended Parkhouse school were women. The only male on the teaching staff was the Headmaster, Mr. Kerr. He taught the older boys.

Having girls in the same class at school was a bit of a novelty. That soon wore off when I discovered that some of the girls were better than me at a number of subjects. Primary school was boring. The pace was geared to that of the slowest student. The goal for the school was to prepare all its students to a standard level in preparation for entry to the High School.

I was 8 years old and preparing to leave for Germany with my parents. My teacher thought it was a wonderful opportunity. My fellow classmates thought I was joining the Gestapo. This led to my first real fight. "You're a Nazi," he said. Though bigger than me I got the first lick in. It was a good one, a right hand flush on the nose. Blood poured out all down the front of his ragged gray pullover. Provocation and departure were not considered valid excuses for violent behavior. After a taste of the "belt" and a strong lecture about my conduct, I bade farewell to Parkhouse School and Scotland. Excited and fearful at the same time, leaving everything and everyone that I knew behind, except Willie of course.

School in Germany was very different. Officers, diplomats and civil servants whom my father drove around, sent their kids to the same school that my brother and I attended. There was only the one Service school in Berlin all British children under the age of 12 attended. If older then you were sent to a boarding school 200 miles away in Willhemshaven.

There were around 40 kids of all ages at the school and the lessons were formal with regular books and so on but there was a large disparity in the levels of education. On occasion Willie and I would take a “day off,” without permission or parental knowledge.
I took German lessons but in truth I wasn’t motivated to the degree that I should have been. My Dad spoke fluent German so why did I have to learn it? Nothing in particular stands out in my memory about my schooling in Berlin. Frankfurt was special in that I was a classmate and friend of Ridley Scott, the now famous movie director. An exceptional drawer, Ridley also told the best stories. Scots and “Geordies” always seem to have a kindred spirit.

British Children Go To School In Berlin

Marilyn Bain, of Kirkcaldy, Fifeshire, and John Wilson, of Arbroath, Forfarshire, at their lessons, and (right) a singing class with Frances Vincent, of Belfast, and William Wilson, of Arbroath, in the front row.

On my return to Arbroath in 1949, there was another change of school, Ladyloan. I don't know why this came about but it didn't matter too much as I was only about eight months away from going to the High School. Willie and I were viewed as Germans on our return! At a school where we knew no one, good humor and the total inability to speak any German, proved to be points in our favor. I made the school football team and passed the tests for the move to the High School.

The High School was divided into grades for those of us coming up from the Primary schools. The highest grade possible for boys to get into was "E." Then there were the lower "F" and "G" grades. These grades all had a technical bent although you had all kinds of subjects such as Geography, Art, PE, English, French and Music. There was one other group for boys called the "L" grade. To this day, I believe it was for literature but don't know how you ever got into that grade. The grades for girls were divided into commercial and domestic.

I guess we were second class citizens really, because almost everyone in the "L's" went on to University after staying at the High School until they were eighteen. We others were all booted out at fifteen with few exceptions. One of those exceptions was my best pal at school Alex Wilson. The teachers always addressed him as Alexander but I always called him Sy. He and I were the two smallest kids in the class. We sat together all the time and frequently were split up for laughing or talking. Sy was the Borough Architect in Forfar the last I heard.

The High school had four wings. Most of my classes were in the North Wing except for Science, Art and PE. You had to know your timetable so as not to miss class. Running between wings, excuses for lateness and other minor offences, were normally punished by belting. My mathematics teacher Mr. Ferguson, "Foggy," was Headmaster of the North Wing and as such was the "master belt giver." Other teachers would send troublesome and tardy students as well as the "poke players" (truant's) to him for punishment. In my last year, we had Algebra for our first period Monday morning and Geometry for our first period after lunch. This meant a parade of miscreants being trooped into the classroom for a variety of crimes. Everything from forging notes purporting to excuse them from school, to threatening a teacher with bodily harm. During these disciplinary sessions we were given book exercises to complete while "Foggy" exercised his formidable punishment skills.

The “belt” was applied normally on the hand or hands for things like being late or not doing homework. It was anything from three to ten lashes, depending on how repetitive an offender you were. For serious offences such as theft, swearing or threatening behavior, the belt was applied to the seat of your pants. We all wore shorts making the tops of the legs very vulnerable. A sudden movement prior to the moment of impact was not recommended!

I had a front row seat for this performance, twice every Monday! After two years of having sampled the “belt” applied by various teachers, I had developed a grading system. “Foggy” was definitely the champion, top of the table. There were always tales about teachers treating their “belts” with various concoctions. This, the theory went, would allow the less physical among them to maximize the pain they could inflict. A one-inch thick, two-inch wide, long leather strap, applied with maximum leverage, does not need to be treated with anything to inflict pain. Trust me!

Neighbors

Whether by accident or design, most families had two children. It worked really well for the accommodations that we lived in. All the buildings were built of red sandstone and had a common entry or passage. The ground floor had two doors off the entry, one on the left and one on the right. Each of these dwellings had two rooms a sitting room and a bedroom. The toilet was outside in the yard and shared with your neighbor. In the back yard, there was the washhouse. The large metal bowl covered by a wooden lid, a mangle with worn wooden rollers, a scrubbing board and a boiler stick were the tools of the trade. You filled the boiler with water then lit a fire in the grate underneath to heat it. Residents used the washhouse in rotation. Each tenant had a specific day for the use of the facility and the drying green. A woman's measure was the whiteness of her washing.

To get to the first floor you passed through an entry then up the outside concrete stairs. The steps were worn and the metal railing was a necessary safety. As on the ground floor, there was a shared outside toilet and a similar layout to that below. A flight of wooden stairs inside the building connected the second floor to the top floor. The stairs led directly to the common toilet between the two attics. Single people often lived in an attic, or a "garrett." The attic had one main room and a very small kitchen area. An advantage to the attic was having the toilet inside the building. A disadvantage was that the roof sloped severely.

The rent was paid to the rent collector or you took a rent book and paid at the solicitor's office. We had running cold water, gas for cooking and lighting with a coal fire for heat and making toast. The attics each had a window, as did the toilet on the middle landing. Dwellings on the other floors had windows in each room. One faced the front of the building and one faced the rear. All the coal cellars were on the ground floor and all had their own key. The tenants shared the cleaning of the common access ways and toilets. There was many a fight over what "clean" actually meant! For some reason the walls of all ground floor "entry's" were painted in red ochre. It made a bright smudge mark on your clothes when you brushed against it. A dead give-away if you had been up to any "hanky panky" in the darkened passageway!

I lived on the middle floor. By good fortune there was no dwelling directly below. Instead there was an entrance for a horse and cart. This unused concrete hall was referred to as the "pend." Apparently our back yard used to be part of an old tannery and the "pend" was used for cart access.

This large entrance, come tunnel, was 15ft long, 6ft wide and 8ft high. Two large wooden doors which bolted together and a much smaller door inset for individual access, closed off the entrance to the street. It proved to be a great benefit to my brother and I, it gave us our own under cover play area. We used it for soccer, basketball, tennis, gang meetings and shelter from the rain. The racket that we made in there by pounding all kinds of balls against that big door drove our next-door neighbors crazy.

The back yard and drying green was huge, just perfect for our England v Scotland "headie" matches. On one side of the yard were the backs of the coal cellars for the next building. The end wall had an unused piece of ground behind it and the third wall was the dividing wall for the next building. Pretty sheltered and we could climb over any one of the walls whenever a crisis arose. Times like being called to go home when you didn't want to go, or to retrieve a miss hit ball.

Our building neighbors were the Penny's and the Carroll's. The Lyall sisters were day neighbors only. They ran the sweetie shop downstairs but didn't live in the building. Dave Penny was a tailor to trade but after returning from WWI he spent most of his time in the pub. His mother was very old, with white unkempt hair and very dirty clothes. She was always dressed in black like a witch. Some unknown tragedy had befallen them but as a kid you don't think about things like that. I never did find out their story. Mr. Carroll worked as a baker. They were a nice family with a daughter Nancy and a son Billy. Nancy was much older than I was and very attractive. She married young and immigrated to New Zealand. Billy was younger than both my brother and I.

The building next to us housed the Mc Farlane's, with two sons Billy and Jackie. The Donahue's lived in the building next to them and had two sons, Jackie and Bobby. Jackie and I were the same age and good pals. Sadly he died from diabetes at the age of eight. In the same entry lived the Watson's, Jim, Ronnie and Bill. Next door to the Watson's was the Cruickshank's with one son, Jimmy.

Directly across the street from us was the shop of Mr. Dave Smart, though neither, he nor his family actually lived in the street. I'm not sure where they lived. He or his wife would arrive in the morning to open and run the shop. He had two daughters but I only remember Elizabeth, the eldest. I met her again briefly while stationed at RAF Leuchars. She was studying at St Andrews along with Sheila, the daughter of our corner butcher, D.Y. Walker. The Walkers didn't live beside us either. Their son, Bruce was a bit older than me. He used to let me play and help out with some of the chores at the shop. The big incentive for me to help was that I could get a good selection of hen's rings. These brightly colored plastic rings were slipped on the hen's leg when young to identify its age. Once a hen reached the butchers, rings were no longer necessary. I used to decorate the handlebars of my message bike with them. A little bit of flash!

Above Mr. Smarts shop, lived the Hannah's., their two sons Norman and Richard were ages with Willie and I. Mr. Hannah was a postman and a part time soccer referee. Adjacent to the Hannah's were the Marr's, one son, Eddie. The Kydd's lived above the Marr's and they had one daughter, Jean. Next to the Kydd's lived the Gunning's. They had two sons, Jack and Bill. Granny's lived either with their families or in an attic. For all these families I recall only four fathers and no grandfathers! WWI left many widows.

Further along Millgate Loan lived the Walkers. Jim was an only son. We both ended up working for the same local firm, G&L Fraser. I met with him many years later in South Africa. The Boath brothers, Ian and Greg, lived next door to Jim. Greg was a dedicated racing cyclist. In the last building on that side lived Bert Herron a professional footballer for Arbroath FC.

There were plenty of shops close by. Lyalls sweetie shop was next door and right across the street, was a fish and chip shop, "The Star." On the corner of the West Port was Robertson's the green grocer and next door to that was the newsagents. Walker's the butcher's was opposite. Craig's china shop was on the other corner and opposite Craigs was a pub, "The Stag." The owner of "The Stag" was Colin Mc Nab. Colin had played for Arbroath FC when they were in the first division and was "capped" for Scotland. He had three children, two daughters and a son. The son Colin and I used to be good pals partly because the grocer's shop that I delivered for was directly below where he lived.

Behind "The Stag" and Craig's were the "linies," railway lines that ran all the way down to the harbor. A great place for adventure was the "linies." Rail cars shunted there for safekeeping were anything but safe. The best fare we could hope for was a car full of monkey nuts. Unshelled peanuts, what a feast! After filling your stomach, you filled your pockets, inside your jumper and anywhere else that might hold more.

In the other direction going south we had the new telephone exchange. Built on the site of the old tannery it was still called the "tanny." Next to the Telephone Exchange was the Labor Exchange. On the corner of Millgate Loan and East Mary Street, was the blacksmith's yard and smithy.

The next shop was Ellis's, which stocked high quality toys and sweets. Bella's was next. She sold everything from newspaper to toilet paper and from birthday cards to postcards. A very kind person was Bella. A few doors down from Bella's lived Andy Swankie, his mother and Granny. His Granny was a clay pipe smoker and rarely left her bed. Her bed was set into an alcove in the main room and you pulled curtains across for

privacy. This style was very common and practical. Lying in one of these beds, staring into the dying embers of a coal fire, gave you an almost primeval feeling. I always imagined faces and shapes in the glowing and slowly shifting coals. A feeling of warmth, security and solitude, all bundled up in your own private little cave.

Further along was Fleming's butcher shop and right next to that was Cargill's. This shop sold groceries and had a little ice cream kiosk that opened directly onto the street. A striped awning caught your attention as you looked ahead. Ice cream made on the premises came in sliders and cones. A three penny cone with "Roy Rogers" sprinkled on it or better still a "99"was a treat worth waiting for. I always thought this was a great idea because you never actually had to go into the shop to get served. Just stop outside on the pavement, order it and watch it being put together. You could start eating it the moment you had it in your hand.

Just a little further on lived Roy and Ian Matthew. In the same building were the Johnson's, whose daughter Leslie was a classmate of mine. There was the North Sea Hotel, the Windmill Hotel, Gayfield and a little further on, the Seaforth Hotel. Tutties Neuk was the closest pub to Gayfield. Lambs garage was opposite Tutties Neuk. Outside the garage, like a sentinel from the past, stood a large glass fuel pump reminding you that it was a long walk to Dundee. The low common, putting greens and various holiday attractions stretched ahead.

The end of 15 Millgate Loan, home sweet home! The pend and Lyall's sweetie shop are demolished and not before time. One of our attics is still visible directly above the Carroll's and Penny's shop. The remaining buildings were gutted and refurbished.

Games

No not really, the games I played were simple and required little or no special equipment. There always seemed to be enough kids to play three or four a side football, which we played in the street. Most of the streets were cobbled and required good balance if you were to stay erect. There were few cars but there was still a steady volume of traffic, buses, delivery carts and of course bicycles.

With only three or four boys,“headie” a form of head tennis, was the choice. Both “headie” and four a side football was played using a tennis ball. When the street was too busy we could play on the grass of our backyards, provided it wasn’t washing day. Mothers and neighbors used to be furious if we played or ran through the washing when it was on the line. Washday meant that everything was boiled, bleached white and then put out to dry on the clothesline, precariously propped up by a “hiser” to catch the “druth.” The sight or sound of bairns on the green was viewed as an imminent disaster site for the newly washed clothes.

On the odd occasion when I teamed up with kids from further along the Loan we would go and play football at the “high common”. When we did this we had to have a full size “fitba.” If you were the owner of such a thing you wielded great authority! The game never, ever, had a finish time or a referee. We played until we could play no more or it was too dark to see. Jackets for goalposts, decisions by consensus and scores of 110 to 109 were not uncommon. There was always the cry of "just one more goal" or "just one more corner." I have been so tired after one of these marathons that I didn't think I would ever find the energy to walk the half-mile home.

My building had its own backyard the other boys who lived on our side of the street had a communal backyard. It was huge but it had an "air raid" shelter built right in the middle of it, which ruined it for football but was a plus for "kick the can." Basically you placed a tin can in an exposed spot and one of the gang was picked to guard it, the rest all ran away and hid. The guardian of the can had to find one of the group and touch him by hand to transfer the guardianship over to that person. Meantime everybody else was trying to sneak up on the can and kick it, so keeping the guardian from getting out of his task.

"Pinner," I have no idea how this game started or where it got its name from but it required a good aim and distance control. You needed a piece of flattened lead, the "pinner," not too big and not too small, about the size of the lid on a tin can. The object of the game was to beat your opponent and in so doing keep his "pinner." The game was that both players started from the same spot and had to pitch his "pinner" onto something made of metal. It didn't have to land on it just touch it and it then lay where it ended up. The opponent then followed suit aiming for another grate or drain away from where the first player had pitched. If you failed to get a touch you were the loser and had to give up your "pinner." The other way to win was to hit your opponents "pinner" with yours. There were plenty of metal objects on the road and on the pavement, manhole covers, drain covers, grates etc. The trick was to stay away from your opponent until you had a good chance of hitting his "pinner." A game of tactics and precision, of course if you were a lousy player you had to keep replacing your "pinner." Buildings back then had plenty of lead!

An evening game was "cheeky mellie." You needed a small nail or pin, a large nail or something similar and some black thread from Mum's sewing basket. You tied the pin and nail together leaving about six inches of thread between them. Then you tied the reel of thread to the large nail.

Now you were ready. Very quietly creep under someone's windowsill and stick the pin or small nail into the putty which kept the glass in. Now you had the large nail hanging down in front of the glass pane, a gentle tug caused the nail to knock against the glass. You waited out of sight for the person in the house to come to the outside door to see what the problem was. Not seeing anyone they would go back inside. You waited for a minute or so and pulled the thread again, after a few times the person was more than agitated. Eventually your laughter gave you away. This game worked really well at night because the street lamps were not well laid out and they were gas lamps, so you couldn't see very well anyway.

Willie and I always had the "pend" to play in and we could play "headie" under cover, basketball with a homemade hoop or just knock a tennis ball against the big door with an old racket. There was one other "game" that my brother and I played in our backyard. Trying to catch pigeons!

Pigeons were everywhere. They lived under the eaves of all the houses. A few men kept lofts full of "doos" for racing. I guessed that some of those racing pigeons got tired of racing and started their own lofts. They were quite big, not as big as wood pigeons but colorful, all shades from white to black, dark brown to almost red. All had one thing in common they had stripes or bars across each wing. There weren't many cats or dogs around but these "doos" were plenty wary, a good challenge for two young, aspiring trappers. Willie and I tried every trick that we knew or had seen at the pictures. Baited traps, nets and every possible combination in between but it was never good enough or fast enough to outsmart them. What we would have done with any that we might have caught I have no idea. Neither of us would have had the courage to kill one.

Apart from money, which we never used for anything else but spending, the currency of youth was mainly, cigarette cards, comics or "bools." Marble's then had better colors than those of today. None had more prestige and value than the "cheeser." This was a special "bool," scarce and not played with, or for, lightly. It was mostly a cloudy white with a red or orange center.

In trades the "cheeser" was worth at least three of anything else. Like all games, they seemed to run in cycles, popular one month and out of favor the next. The seasons of course had an influence on games because we never got to play indoors.

In the summer we would build "bogies." A washed up fish box, wheels from an abandoned pram or scooter, nails and some ingenuity. No brakes a piece of rope tied to the two front wheels to act as a steering mechanism. Why no one was ever injured or even killed in one of these contraptions is a miracle. We would launch ourselves down the Mount Zion Brae, which was very steep, and across the main road to safety. All on the chance that the boy at the bottom of the brae could judge the flow of traffic correctly!

The winter months opened up new avenues to explore. Ice skating, a sledge or sled, homemade of course and snowball fights. Ice skating, was always done at the Castle like, water tower or "Lochy." Our ice skates clamped onto your boots and for this a special key was required. There were two problems with this arrangement. The first was not to lose the key, which adjusted the mechanism that made the skates fit your boots. Second, if you put them on tight enough to stay on, you could ruin your boots by splitting the sole!

The studs in the soles of your boots and the steel clips at the toe and on the heel not only extended the life of the footwear but would give off a great amount of sparks when used as emergency brakes on your bike or bogie. Walking any distance wearing these boots was like weight training for your legs, you felt like a horse, clip, clopping along.

Wellington boots on the other hand had no studs, were very light on the feet and could be adapted to serve any number of different roles. They were waterproof, allowing you to run through puddles or play at the beach and not get your feet wet. You could wash them, polish them and make them look like a gentleman's riding boot. Best of all you could turn the tops down, showing the white lining and pretend that you were one of the Three Musketeers. Lastly you could wear socks with holes in them and nobody would be any the wiser, especially Mother, she hated darning socks!

Holidays

Visitors were in abundance in the summer as they came to town for their holidays. I never gave any thought to living in a holiday resort. To me it was just my hometown; I took it for granted that everybody lived like me. The summer holidays were always looked forward to. I still had my jobs but no school. The water was always a magnet although I was never comfortable close to deep water and in my case that was anything more than 5 feet! Having said that I used to spend day after day fishing at the dock gates where a fall into the dock would certainly require the ability to swim assuming you were able,

Watching the fishing boats come in or watching the dredger at work was two other favorite pastimes. I thought that running that dredger would be a great job. It was a boat built specifically for the purpose of clearing channels for boats by digging underwater with a continuous chain of buckets. The buckets tipped the muck and sludge from the bottom of the harbor into a special tank built into the boat. When full it would sail out of the harbor and drop its load a couple of miles off shore. It was the noisiest, smelliest and dirtiest boat in the harbor!

If you needed to earn money you could spend a few weeks picking strawberries or raspberries. I did this once or twice but it was too fiddly for me, I never seemed to be able to get into a rhythm.

You were left to pick at your own pace, no quotas or anything. If you didn't pick and weigh in your bucket, you didn't get paid. This activity just didn't have the discipline and control of the "tatties" maybe that's why I never made any money at it. It lacked the spirit or camaraderie, of being part of a group, because it was different people every day. There was no set starting time or finishing time. No transportation, no set pick up points just got on your bike and pedaled. However it was a good place to meet girls! Holiday girls would go to the "berry picking" to make spending money.

The beach played a major role in most activities and it was only a 10 minute walk, from where I lived. My mother always liked to work on her tan so she was always ready to go to the beach. The "slippy," the lifeboat slipway was her favorite spot even though we used to get caught by the tide regularly.

A blanket to sit on, a towel to dry you with and a vacuum flask with tea, maybe even a biscuit. These were the days of the knitted bathing costume! When wet, the wool got heavier, coupled with gravity this meant that you needed two hands to preserve your dignity. Adam had more reliable coverage!

There was always something exciting about walking the beach early in the morning when no one else was about. It made me feel like an explorer of sorts. All kinds of stuff would wash up, boxes, bottles, dead birds, dead fish and a number of more intimate items. The rocks, at "Inchy,"

(Inchcape) a small area of the beach, were always exciting to look over. You could find shoals of small fish packed in pools as the tide had turned and trapped them. Crabs were always hiding under the small rocks. Most exciting of all you could walk out to the Protection Wall that guarded the southern part of the harbor entrance. Climbing up this wall was a big challenge for a little guy like me. It was always covered in seaweed and seagull droppings, very slippery. The sea gulls would shriek at you as you carefully walked the one hundred yards to the end of the wall. Only at certain times of the year was this possible because of the tides.

My mother had friends who lived in Glasgow and when they came on holiday it was great fun. They were always playing cards. Find the Lady, or "Horsey" and Twenty-One are the games I remember. The odd half crown slipped into your hand with the proviso that you don't tell mum. Ice cream, sunny days, no worries, fish and chips, picnics, and walks to the "flairs" at Auchmithie. I was so tired with all the walking and fresh air that at the end of the day I was asleep before my head hit the pillow. However I might be woken up when they all came back from the pub. Seemed like every night ended up with a joke session or a song, often both. It was fun to have so many adults together, all hell bent on having a good time and just mucking in. Willie and I slept on the floor to accommodate them all.

Picnics to places like Carmylie or Inverkeilor were invariably interrupted by rain. Only places that had a hall were ever used for these summer excursions. Three legged races, wheelbarrow races and sack races were all standard picnic activities. No other brown bag lunch has ever tasted as good since.

During any holiday period Willie and I would go to the cattle mart on a Wednesday morning. It wasn't just cattle that were auctioned but sheep as well. The cattle coming down the street from the railway station and being herded towards the mart always preceded this auction. It was great fun, cows and sheep crapping all over the street and people running to get out of the way. Men with sticks shouting and trying to get the animals herded together before penning them at the mart. I used to go inside to the ring, watching and listening to the farmers bid for the animals. The auctioneer would start "blethering," a small pause followed a rap of his cane on the rail would indicate that a sale had been made. The real spectacle began after the mart closed. Some animals had to be herded to the "skemells," (slaughter house) about three streets away. This often turned out to be Arbroath's version of "running with the bulls."

There was the Arbroath Pageant Parade, which coincided with the peak holiday period and always attracted a large crowd. Company floats, the Salvation Army Band and the local vet dressed as "Robert the Bruce" riding a horse that had the Scottish flag draped over its back. The parade started at "Auld Shore Head" and continued all the way up

the High Street to the Abbey. There were always collections being taken for all sorts of local groups, this entailed 4 to 6 people carrying a stretched out blanket and bystanders pitched coins into it. Clydesdales from many farms, all with gleaming harness wear and beautifully groomed were always part of the parade.

Around the early fifties there were "Extravaganzas" held at the Victoria Park a natural amphitheater and these were wonderful events with all kinds of acts including trapeze artists, sideshows and numerous other activities including a huge firework display in the evening. A Publicity Council was appointed and tried very hard to get visitors to come to holiday in Arbroath. The bathing pool was used for many events such as the Miss Arbroath Beauty Contest and dances in the evening.

Christmas was in truth pretty miserable. As we didn't have TV yet all we knew of toys was what we saw in shop windows, there was little advertising?

Woolworth's was the biggest store in the town and it sold everything you needed for Christmas apart from the food. Yule's was the next biggest shop which specialized in books and annuals. The clue to the near arrival of Christmas was the Santa like figure that used to appear in Clark's the cyclist shop window. Clad in a red suit and mounted on a gleaming new bicycle, this automaton would "pedal" day and night, untiringly. The clothes were just long enough to cover the battery, motor and gears used to power the back wheel.

To expect a new bike for Christmas was aiming pretty high, but HP was an option for your parents. Clark's also had a Christmas club, which allowed you to start saving months before Christmas, so that you could build up enough money to buy something. These bikes were very staid and heavy by today's standards. Some had a three-speed gear fitted or a dynamo. Lights front and back were normally battery powered with the front light clipping onto a special bracket on the handlebars. But if you had a dynamo the lights were actually bolted to the bike! Like millions of others, I never did get a new bike for Christmas.

Remembering that the war years allowed little money for frivolous things, the end of the war saw changes in many things, including toys. Toys were mostly passive, there was no action unless you moved them by hand, or you wound a spring to provide power to the clockwork mechanism. Imagination that was the key to Christmas toys! Jig Saw puzzles were a real good gift, books, and board games of all types mostly played with dice also were a good choice. Ludo was very popular as was Snakes and Ladders. As the fifties began, things like chemistry sets and Mechanno sets became available. There were the old standbys, kaleidoscopes, spinning tops that made a sound like a siren, and of course sweets, fruit and nuts. If you were really lucky a "Broon's Book" or an "Oor Wullie" annual would appear in your stocking.

As limited as our Christmas's were, we always had a nice meal and naturally Christmas crackers. The small toys inside those crackers were really good quality. Games shaped like a small round tin with a clear top looking down on a picture that had a number of holes cut out. There were little metal balls inside that you had to fit into the holes. This skill, when mastered, would have been most useful to an aspiring brain surgeon! Small frames with sliding tiles, which had the letters of the alphabet or numbers on them, required manipulation, patience and perseverance to get them into the correct order. There was always paper hat's, made of brightly colored tissue paper and inside each one, a slip of paper with a joke printed on it. "What's black and white and red all over?" Of course, a newspaper.

New Year was always bigger than Christmas in Scotland but it was an adult thing. Parties, kissing and drinking, not that there's anything wrong with any of that! Willie and I went "first footing" from an early age. You wrapped everyday things like a tin of something, a bar of something or a packet of something, in a colored piece of paper and that would be your "first footing" gift, a head of dark hair, your first footing gift or a piece of coal was all it took. Of course if you happened to have a bottle of something that didn't hurt either.

The New Year was "brought in" at Kirk Square beside the steeple, in the heart of the town. A countdown was followed by a loud cheer and the deep and sincere hope that things really would be better in the coming year. First footing was not limited to New Year's Day it depended on which day of the week it landed on and your physical perseverance. Men often were gone for days, lost in a drunken fog, fed by well-meaning friends and sleeping where they fell.

As part of the "first footing" visit you were expected to perform some act of entertainment before you could enjoy the fare provided. Each generation had their particular rendering, be it poetry, humor or song. This was a great learning experience for me and it provided a means of passing on old words, verse and songs. Favorite's such as "We' re No Awa Tae Bide Awa," "I Belong to Glasgow," "Johnny Scobie," "Auld Reekie" and the more modern "A Scottish Soldier," made popular by the town's own, Andy Stewart. There were many others, which now only come to mind when I hear the music being played. For me it was a window into adulthood, stories of days gone by, absent friends, songs that I had never heard before and watching grown men cry. “Happy New Year,” hope sprang eternal.

Jobs

My first paid employment was the "tattie holidays." There is a misnomer if ever I heard one. How the word holiday ever became associated with picking potatoes is beyond me. This six-week break allowed children to assist farmers to bring in their crop. Only the needy actually engaged in this activity, which meant it fell fair and square into the Wilson family court. A yearly activity, which was in, mothers "something will turn up" category. She never actually went. My brother took over my morning and afternoon jobs so I could earn the bigger money.

School children and family members were picked up at 6am at designated street corners, by open lorries or tractors with flat trailers and were taken out to the fields. As an early riser I didn't find this a hardship but it didn't help my attitude any if I let my mind wander on that 20-minute ride. I thought of many things on those rides, none of which endeared me to the task at hand. As hard as it was to go, doing "a runner," only increased the workload on those that remained. Of course you had nowhere to go and no means of getting there. Going home was out of the question hard earned money had been spent in preparing you and the food you carried for the day's work. Better to have lost a limb or have contracted some life threatening disease before you tried that one on.

You had your morning and afternoon breaks in the field and lunch at the farmhouse. Food and a warm drink were never more satisfying. The day was measured by the number of "drills" that had to be picked. If you needed to relieve yourself there were no such things as portable toilets you had to find a convenient hedge or hollow. For the women this was a source of constant complaint. "Piecee time," the morning break that is, normally came after picking about 8 drills, lunch break followed after another 8. After lunch it was the same routine until 4 o'clock, by then you were on your knees crawling. Time to go home!

As miserable as it could be, there was camaraderie to it and the tiredness of a hard day's work did give a feeling of self-worth. But there were other valuable lessons to be learned. I don't know whether it was being close to "mother earth" or the fresh air but sex was never far from the conversation. Lunch hours spent in the barn was a very popular pastime. Not being old enough to participate, my pals and I reveled in the role of spoilers or is the proper word voyeurs?

Dirty songs, dirty jokes and seeing adults in unfamiliar roles were all part of the indelible experience.

Horses were used for most of the heavy chores on the farm. Big gentle Clydesdales pulled the chain digger with steady, plodding accuracy. "tattie howking" was in October and November, often with frost on the ground! The "tatties" truly were a godsend to many families. The pay was good, it was honest work and it provided money to clothe kids for school with maybe a little something left over for Christmas. Saturday was a half-day and also payday. It was a great thrill to hear the Grieve call your name and then hand you a small brown packet with folding money in it! It felt good to have that money to take home and I got enough of it for my limited life style. It was amazing how quickly the dirt and the tiredness disappeared on Saturday night. Washed and all dressed up, money in my pocket, off to the pictures I would go.

My regular paid employment started when I was 12 years old. My parents' divorce proceedings were then in the final stages, my father and Germany were only memories. As "the man of the house" until I left for the RAF, I always had two jobs, one before school and another after school. My first after school job was at the Co-Operative Society, the "Sochie" as it was commonly referred to. The only reason that I wanted to work there was because they had a system for handling customer payments that was unique and it fascinated me. Not the best motivation for taking the job but certainly an added attraction.

A counter clerk would fill your order and that meant everything from slicing ham to cutting blocks of cheese from a big round. Tinned meats and bacon were placed onto a spiked stainless steel plate that was pulled across a rotating super sharp blade about

12 inches in diameter and operated by a handle. Cheese and all other kinds of bulk items came in cloth sacks or chests, even sides of meat and pork came wrapped in muslin. Tea came from India in 3 feet square plywood chests lined with silver foil. When empty, tea chests were popular storage items. Flour came in 100lb sacks. Cereals and sugar was weighed, on scales, in front of the customer. All weights were in pounds and ounces. With almost everything in bulk, weighing and bagging were important.

Brown paper bags of various sizes were the standard. No plastic or polythene yet and few prepackaged goods. Paper bags were easily torn or punctured, ensuring that the floor of the shop would become messy. The answer to this problem was to put damp sawdust onto the wooden floor to contain and absorb spillage. It also prevented dust and dirt from getting into the air.

The sawdust was swept up every day, sometimes more than once and was laid down fresh in the morning. That was part of my first job as was cleaning up any spillage or breakage. I should mention that I was only 5 foot tall and stayed that way until I was almost eighteen. Height or the lack of it meant that I always had to try and do things a bit better than the bigger kids. Trying to reach higher or lift things heavier than I could carry would eventually lead to my undoing.

Getting back to the main reason for wanting to work there, the payment system! There were wire cables strung above the floor to every counter in the store and they all terminated at a glass, fronted booth,

situated in the middle of the store where only one person handled all the money. Getting the money to that one person was the trick and that was my fascination. Viewed from the floor and looking up to the roof, it was like a spider's web with the glass booth taking the place of the spider. Each counter position had a wire cable terminated above it and each cable had a wooden cup with a screw top on it. The clerk would write up the order, mark the price against each item, total it by hand then put the piece of paper that he had written everything on, into the cup along with the customer's money. The cup was then screwed in to the lid and the clerk would pull a handle to propel the wooden cup all the way to the cashier in the booth. Magic!

Counter clerks were expected to tally the customer's bill on the spot and in plain sight of the customer .We did not use the abacus in Scotland!

Pricing and totaling of the bill was done with a pencil on the paper that the customer's purchase was wrapped in. Should you think pricing and totaling the bill a trivial task consider. Bulk goods were priced by the pound but customers often bought by the quarter pound. An item that sold for 17pence per pound would cost 4 pence and one farthing per quarter pound! There were twenty shillings in a pound and there were twelve pennies in a shilling. There were twenty-one shillings in a guinea, four farthings in a penny and thirty penny's in half a crown. Six half pennies made three pence, ten thrupenny bits made half a crown as did five tanners. There were four half crowns in ten bob, five two-shilling pieces in ten bob and two ten bob notes equaled a pound. Got it?

Compounding the division and multiplication skills required, was the weight system. Sixteen ounces equaled one pound and fourteen pounds equaled one stone, a measure greater than that was outside the realm of my comprehension and certainly wouldn't have fitted into a brown paper bag.

The point being that it wasn't easy to be a counter clerk. You needed other skills apart from being good with numbers. The additional skills required were not taught at school. You had to smile a lot, have good local knowledge, have some degree of salesmanship, like people and have a little bit of gossip to pass along. My ambition to rise to the heady position of counter clerk with the Co-Op was crushed along with the twenty, one-pound glass jars of jam, dropped from my keeping to the floor. They wouldn't even let me clean it up. The sack, the bag, the elbow, on your bike! Never again was I to experience this ignominy, onward and upward for me and from being an even five feet tall that wasn't too difficult.

Morning delivery jobs fell into three categories, papers, milk or rolls. All these jobs had one thing in common, time pressure!. Milk bottles were heavy and had no real upside. I mean how much milk can you drink? Rolls, bread rolls that is, are made in a bakery, bakeries are nice and warm in the morning and there is always plenty of free stuff to take home. The down side is that tips are lousy, as no one ever sees you. That left newspapers! Now if you screw up and forget someone or leave the wrong paper they do get upset but it is not the end of the world. If you forget to leave rolls for someone they can't have breakfast and the same goes for milk. Paper delivery seemed the least work with the best tip potential. I did deliver rolls for a year but newspapers were my preference.

The morning newspapers were dropped from the northbound train at six am. My job was to pick them up and carry them back to the shop. Because they only serviced their own locale most shops had only one paperboy. Once back in the shop you had to count every one of the papers in the bundle that you had carried from the station. There was only one local daily The Courier but there were a number of national papers that were popular, The Daily Mail, The Daily Express and The Daily Record. You had maybe twenty minutes in the warm shop to count and sort them for your deliveries.

As the delivery boy you had a book. The shop owned the book and it was updated by the shop to reflect changes in customers and their wants. However it was your job to make sure that you left the shop with the correct number of papers and magazines. Different days called for certain magazines. The major problem was putting the exact amount of each in your bag after checking the book for changes. exact amount of each in your bag after checking the book for changes.

Common sense and expediency prevailed. As you walked your route you delivered papers to the customers who lived closest to the shop first, that way your bag got lighter as you moved along your route. If you finished your route and you had papers left over, you had a problem. If you got to your last customer, always the one furthest from the shop and you had no paper left or you had the wrong paper left, you had another problem. You could be as creative as you liked about what you said when you got back to the shop, if you said anything at all! But someone was going to be upset and would come in and complain. Lesson learned, people that complain don't tip!

Newspapers are educational. I picked stuff up without even thinking about it. I increased my vocabulary, gleaned valuable geographical knowledge and was kept up to date on the latest football stories. All this and I got paid for it as well! Another upside of working for a newsagent was that you could read almost anything for free, if you had the time. The most important thing to me was that I got to order stuff, like my comics. I had to pay for them but I could order them. That may not seem such a big deal but there were only three comics that I really liked and they were The Wizard, which came out on Tuesday and then there was The Hotspur and The Rover, which came out on Thursday. There were no pictures or cartoon drawings, these comics were full of stories about such wonderful characters as "Alf Tupper, Tough of the Track," "Matt Bradock, Master Pilot," "Limp Along Leslie" and many others.

When a newsagent sold out of something like that, he was sold out, there were no more, you had to go to other shops and try there. Now as I worked after school, I had no time to search around, so being able to order my comics was a big plus. Why you might ask wouldn't I just order them anyway? Newsagents hate having dated merchandise sitting on the shelf unsold and they certainly wouldn't trust any twelve-year old kid to come in every week and pay for his order. The money was taken out of my wages.

A "message boy" with a decent shop, got a bike! Why groceries were always referred to as "messages," I have no idea. The message bike had a space for a large basket over the small front wheel. On the bar of the bike there was a plate, which had the name of the shop, painted on it. You could use the bike for school as well as for work a big plus, especially if you had a morning job as well. Wearing boots helped develop very strong legs. Coupled with my short stature and ready smile I had the attributes paramount for a well tipped grocery delivery boy.

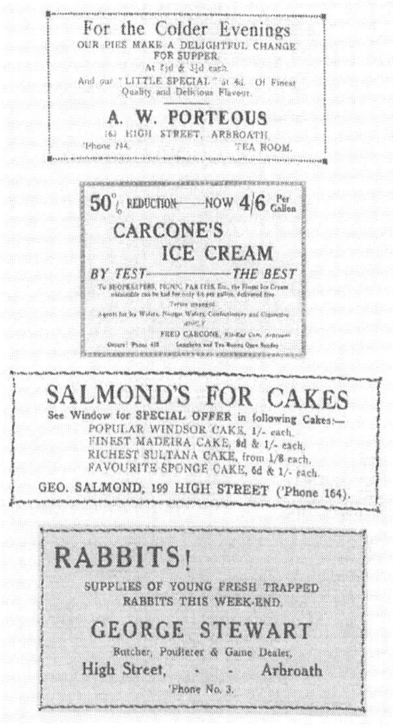

A home phone was a luxury that was enjoyed by business owners, doctors and other professional people. Only three digit numbers were required to service our whole community! At the shop where I worked the only area of town that phoned in orders was the West End, the posh end, where there were no shops. Not everyone who lived at the West End was well off but they tended to be much like most of us today, busy people with limited time. From where I lived and worked the only way to the West End was literally and physically all uphill. On a cobbled street, with rain pouring down and with that little wheel under a heavy basket, life could get interesting in a hurry. I fell more than once, back to the shop my tail between my legs. Regroup, repack and back out again!

I have mentioned tips more than once in this chapter, with good reason. My pay from both jobs went straight to my mother to help keep the household afloat. Now I didn't mind that, I thought it was how it should be. My spending money came from my tips! Without my spending money the picture houses and sweetie shops would surely have gone into recession.

My employer for my after school job, George Mathieson, was a great guy and gave me plenty of encouragement and support. I stayed with George for three years as an after-school job and full time for the six months prior to me joining the Boys Service. He didn't want to lose me but he did want me to better myself. George knew my mother quite well and I suspect extended her a bit of credit now and then.

An after school job was a necessity and there were options. Was the job something that would help you when you applied for an apprenticeship or was it just a means of earning a wage? There wasn't a job in Arbroath that I knew of and wanted, not one! I had ambition, no real brains but I had ambition but I wanted more. Germany had opened my eyes to other worlds.

I saw good people get stuck in jobs that I knew I would hate within months. Get a job, get married, have kids and by the time you are twenty five years old your life is mapped out for you, not for me.

World War II

In the USA when we mention "The War," it is not usually WWII. This is not so in the UK. WWII was a watershed event, its beginning saw a country hung over from a Victorian era, with illusions of Empire. Insular, with an attitude that everything that was British was best. I believed that for a long time!

Prior to WWII, travel within the country was limited to almost regional locations. Travel abroad truly was a rich man's domain, when the war was over that changed. Aircraft were a common sight in the skies the "common man" had traveled to places he hardly even knew existed before the war. Horizons were expanded the genie was out of the bottle. The British Empire of Victoria was being dismantled; independence was the order of the day.

For those who had to go to war and were fortunate enough to survive, the country and the town they came back to was a different place to the one they had left. Coming home and trying to adjust to a humdrum way of life was impossible for some and not enough for many. Fallen comrades, lost brothers and sisters, parents who had grown old in their enforced absence, everything looked smaller and older. There were many changes and the country was on the move.

What I didn't know or understand was why, as we had won, was there still so little food, poor living conditions and no work for all these men who I had never seen before? My world had very few men in it. Most of my pals had fathers in the service and mothers working in men's jobs. The only men around were old, medically unfit or had special skills that were required for the war effort. My schoolteachers were mostly women. Not too many role models there for small boys, who wanted to shoot Germans, gun down the Luftwaffe or slaughter Japs.

I was too young to remember seeing the men go to war but I do remember them coming home. Like many other children my link with my father was a photograph that was looked at every day. I didn't really know who he was. That changed dramatically in late 1945 when fathers and sons started coming home. In the time that they had been away families had made adjustments and in the odd case had actually increased! We had street parties, banners strung out across the street and all kinds of "Welcome Home" signs and placards. Flags and singsongs with food drink and fruits, some of which were completely alien to me such as bananas.

It didn't last long slipping back into the pre-war routine was an impossibility things had gone too far. Men wanted their jobs back, women wanted to keep working and retain a degree of independence. Old industries had gone and new industries had sprung up. New skills were needed to compete in this new democracy. Those who had not gone to war were well off and had the new skills and positions of authority. The young men who weren't old enough to go to war had filled many positions that would normally have gone to more mature people. Remember you left school at 14 years of age then and did an apprenticeship of 3 to 5 years before becoming a journeyman. No GI Bill here for all the men that had served their country and little monetary compensation to the wives whose husbands, sons and daughters had made the supreme sacrifice. The wartime industries were no longer required, the country was broke and owed money. But of course I didn't understand any of that then.

The men all looked old, even in their thirties and early forties and more, they acted old. My father did not fit this mold nor did my mother. On his return from Germany my father spent a few weeks at home before he had to report back to Edinburgh for demobilization (demob). This entailed handing over your service kit and uniform for a new suit, shoes, hat and a small amount of money.

Having a man around the house was strange. I say house but it was really only two rooms with an outside toilet. As young as I was, my mother had often asked me for help as well as for my opinion. That all changed when father came home. We didn't know him and he didn't know us. If I had been older maybe I would have been more understanding. Coming back to reality after being caged up for years, dreaming of coming home to things as they used to be, it must have been hard.

Having said that, later events proved that coming home for him was a bigger adjustment than any of us could have imagined! I never heard my father talk of the war or relay any feelings or opinions about it.

Politics was a subject that never came up in our house, religion on the other hand did come up every once in a while. Raised as a Protestant I never did understand how there could be only one God but so many different religions. My father never could give me an answer. He always indicated that it would unacceptable if I were to grow up and marry a Catholic. Where this came from I can only guess but probably it was a throwback to his Glasgow days or his Northern Irish roots. For me it was never an issue.

Our domestic situation didn't seem to change much prior to our leaving for our 3-year stay in Germany. Father was never really happy, didn't settle at all and spent a lot of time in the pub. He had a temper to, but for some reason my brother always seemed to get the brunt of it. It always hurt me a bit, to think of all the things my brother and I did, collect salvage for the war effort, prayed at night for our father's return and yet things never turned out to be as good as we were sure they would be. Our situation was no better or worse than thousands of others faced with the same challenges. The war had changed everything, outlook, attitude and expectations.

Travel

Apart from a train trip to Greenock when I was about 6 or 7 years old the furthest I had been was to Dundee. A full sixteen miles away! This was an age when commercial air travel was virtually non-existent, everyone traveled by bus or train. Cars were a novelty. Anyone lucky enough to own one couldn't get petrol to run it during the war, and after the war petrol was still strictly rationed. I didn't know one person who owned a car! There were bus services, the main one being Bluebird that ran from Arbroath to Dundee and back. It seemed they stopped at every farmhouse between the two places. There was no service after ten pm. Farm workers owned bicycles!

My real travel started when I reached the grand old age of eight. When the war ended and my father came home he was offered a job as a chauffeur by the Control Commission for Germany (CCG). This was a Commission whose job it would be to govern and set up the administrative framework to allow Germany to get back on its feet. I was going to travel to, Germany and live in Berlin!

On the night train from Arbroath to London we had a sleeper car to ourselves! Arriving at King's Cross, a man dressed in a spotless white starched jacket knocked on the door with tea and biscuits. Next was the tube to Waterloo station. My only knowledge of the underground was what I had seen at the pictures. In my mind I could see a leading man stepping from the carriage with great ease and balance prior to the train stopping. I should have paid closer attention to his feet instead of his looks. I put the wrong foot down first, stumbled and promptly mowed down a number of waiting passengers. God bless them, they broke my fall and helped me up as well!

The boat train in the afternoon took us on the short journey to Harwich. There we boarded a ship, which took us on an overnight trip to the Hook of Holland. From there it was the train to Berlin, via Arnhem and Hanover. These were names I had only heard on the radio or heard from the newsreels at the pictures. I was an international traveler! My father had to leave ahead of us so we traveled on our own. Apart from about half the BAOR (British Army On the Rhine) giving us a helping hand, I naturally assumed, as the recently deposed "man of the house," that I did it all.

It was a wonderful experience for two young boys. I was totally unaware of the momentous events that had happened in the places we passed through. Insulated from the loss of life and the hardship being suffered by millions across the continent, my head was filled with Hollywood movies, newsreel clips and fanciful tales from the comics of the day. I had visions of spies and SS officers hiding everywhere just waiting for Willie and me to catch them.

Our three- year stay in Germany provided us with lots of travel and in many different forms of transport. The 'U' Bahn in Berlin was similar to the underground in London. As children of the occupying forces we had a special badge, which we wore, that allowed us to travel on public transport for free. There were the tramcars in Berlin also which we had never seen before and rode with great abandon. I was given two cigarettes everyday as fare for going to and coming from school by taxi.

Our father, had the use of the staff car when not on duty and we drove everywhere in that car. A big Humber Snipe with official plates. When our stay in Germany was over, we retraced our steps for the journey home. The route was the same but somehow everything had changed. A journey in reverse but seen through very different eyes. There were still the Blue, Green and Red trains but it had become a well-established routine. When I was in the RAF and posted to Germany many years later, this system was still in place.

This all seems very small stuff when compared to today's travel. But for an eight year old, in 1946 this was heady stuff. There were few commercial airlines, no jets and it took six days to sail to America. Most adults, apart from those who had gone to war, never traveled more than a few miles from home and holidays away from home or abroad, were out of reach for most families.

My next train journey was also a landmark. I was 15 and had applied to join the RAF Boys Service. The entrance examinations were to take place at RAF Cosford, which is just outside Wolverhampton in England. No sleeper for this trip, they started the conditioning process early. There were two hundred and fifty of us from all over the UK trying to fill 60 spots. A Flight Sergeant with a clipboard greeted us and started to call out our names. I never realized until then what a disadvantage it was to have a surname starting with a W. Apart from those of Polish or Greek extraction I was at the tail end of every line! The trip was to be repeated three months later when I was notified that I had been accepted.

The only other travel that I can recall was going to play football for the Arbroath Schoolboys at Methil, in Fife, about 60 miles from Arbroath. There was no Tay Road Bridge then so we stayed on the bus as the ferry took us from Dundee to Wormit. Looking out the bus window, my confidence was not boosted by the sight of the river lapping against the stumps of the ill-fated, first Tay Rail Bridge. They were clearly in view, as they still are today.

Dundee car and passenger ferry

If you wanted to travel from North to South, trains were the answer. If you wanted to travel by train going east to west you became very familiar with Crewe station, the saying being that if you stood long enough at Crewe station you would meet everyone you ever knew. From Carlisle to Carstairs and from London to Llanelli, the warm waiting rooms were a great comfort regardless of class.

Germany

It was February 1946, about 9 months after the official end of the war in Europe. The excitement of traveling to Berlin was tempered quickly by the reality of war, seeing buildings flattened and cities decimated. Old and young alike, pulled, pushed, fought and begged for food. Insulated behind the security of a train window I was shocked.my knowledge of war had come from newsreels.

Each Haupt Bahnhoff that we passed through or stopped at was a mess. Glass roofs shattered, debris, track and carriages piled high and yet the train kept on going. At every stop there were people begging for something or wanting to sell something. I don't know what I expected to see, but this wasn't it. Every building was pock marked by bullets, hardly a

window with an unbroken pane. Stacks of salvaged bricks lined each street or what was left of a street. Tramcars ran where it seemed impossible to thread a way through the rubble.

We lived in a compound and I mean a compound, surrounded by barbed wire and a wooden fence. Access was through a main gate that was manned at all times by Military Policemen. Willie and I thought it was to keep us from breaking out but it was supposed to keep any of the local Germans from breaking in.

We had to go to the gate in the morning and wait for a taxi to take us to school, which was about 5 miles away. We paid in cigarettes, as German money was worthless. The script money, BAF's (British Allied Forces) was only negotiable within the service community. With plastic "coins" and paper notes in pastel colors it looked like Monopoly money.

When not at school I had a tremendous amount of freedom. Thinking back my parents should have been a lot more concerned about where my brother and I were and what we were doing. Our little metal Union Jack badge, always pinned to our person was

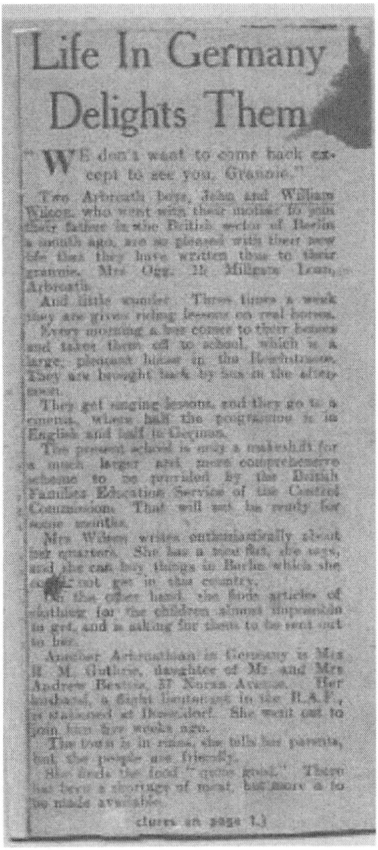

Life In Germany Delights Them

"WE don't want to come back except to see you, Grannie."

Two Arbroath boys, John and William Wilson, who went with their mother to join their father in the British sector of Berlin a month ago, are so pleased with their new life that they have written thus to their grannie, Mrs Ogg, [illegible] Millgate Loan, Arbroath.

And little wonder. Three times a week they are given riding lessons on real horses.

Every morning a bus comes to their homes and takes them off to school, which is a large, pleasant house in the [illegible]. They are brought back by bus in the afternoon.

They get singing lessons, and they go to a cinema, where half the programme is in English and half in German.

The present school is only a makeshift for a much larger and more comprehensive scheme to be provided by the British Families Education Service of the Control Commission. That will not be ready for some months.

Mrs Wilson writes enthusiastically about her quarters. She has a nice flat, she says, and she can buy things in Berlin which she [illegible] get in this country.

[illegible] the other hand, she finds articles of clothing for the children almost impossible to get, and is asking for them to be sent out to her.

Another Arbroathian in Germany is Mrs H. M. Guthrie, daughter of Mr and Mrs Andrew Beattie, [illegible] Nursa Avenue. Her husband, a flight lieutenant in the R.A.F., is stationed at [illegible]. She went out to join him five weeks ago.

The town is in ruins, she tells her parents, but the people are friendly.

She finds the food "quite good." There has been a shortage of meat, but more is to be made available.

[illegible] on page 1.)

always pinned to our person, and was our passport to freedom. Can you imagine two little boys roaming around, searching through bombed buildings for whatever of interest they could find? What the German people must have thought, seeing two little boys with no apparent concern for their plight, running around doing pretty much what they liked, I can only imagine.

The article above was at best poetic license. Horse riding! Horses I would have remembered. Can you imagine what our old neighbors and classmates must have thought after reading this? Britain was still heavily rationed while we were living it up. The description of our accommodation was right on. We also had a piano in the living room but of course none of us could play it!

We lived on Kaiserdam Strasse which ran right through the middle of Berlin, It had two lanes in both directions divided by a median which used to have trees. Firewood turned out to be more important than the scenery.

Our building had an elevator and we lived on the top floor. It really wasn't an apartment it had two floors, electric light, a kitchen and a balcony. The street ran to the French War Memorial turning there to the Brandenburg Gate, about four miles away. This was the boundary of the Russian Sector. Going in the other direction you would pass our school and then the Olympic Stadium would come into view. The huge Berlin radio station tower was almost directly behind our building.

The Brandenburg Gate is mostly remembered today as the site where the Berlin Wall came down. In 1946 it was a landmark in the City that defined the boundary of one of the occupying powers, Russia! Berlin was a divided City with four sectors, British, French, American and Russian. You could not move freely between them!

As my father drove an official car this was not a problem but civilians could not cross between sectors without passes. Even then the people living in the Russian sector wanted out. The film "The Big Lift" depicts economic and living conditions perfectly..

At this time the city of Berlin was a divided city an island, surrounded by countries occupied and controlled by Russia, an outpost of democracy which was not self-sufficient, a weakness that the Russians would later try to exploit. Food, petrol and most other goods were readily available in every sector except the Russian sector. As young as I was, the economic power of a pair of nylons, a bar of chocolate or a pack of cigarettes, was not wasted on me. The sheer joy of being able to go into the American PX or the soda fountain was like a scene from a movie. If only the German people watching had known, this was as much of a dream to me as it must have seemed to them. Comic books, candy bars that I had only seen in magazines, Bazooka chewing gum, Pepsi Cola, milk shakes, my very first banana split! This was a golden time for Willie and me.

As good as it was for me, it was desperate for the civilian population. Martial law was the law. Incidents between the occupying troops were to be avoided at all costs. Civilians, particularly young women, paid a high price for that dictum. From the balcony of our flat I would watch columns of trucks driving past on their way to the Russian sector. Often a truck would suddenly stop and snatch a woman from the street. I didn't really understand what that was about, but I knew it wasn't good. The Russian troops were feared by the Germans and with good reason. The security of living in this divided city was soon to be tested.

There were invariably incidents at the checkpoints, Checkpoint Charlie being the most famous but these normally blew over with apologies from both sides. The bigger picture was that all roads into Berlin were in what is now called East Germany and ruled by a puppet communist government. The British, French and Americans depended on road, river and rail transport to supply almost all their requirements for food and fuel. The Russians did not assist with that in any way quite the contrary. There were two Berlin Airports, Tempelhof that was under the control of the Americans and Gatow under the control of the British. I used to go to both with my father, when he had to collect something.

The Russians blockaded the city the second winter I was there and it was a bitter winter. Denied access to roads, rail and river the only way it seemed to break this deadlock was to abandon the City. An alternative was to attempt to supply the city by air!

This was a task of monumental proportions if in fact it could be done at all. Nothing on this scale had ever been attempted before. Everything from sacks of coal to sacks of flour was flown in. The Berlin Airlift was a major success due to a lot of factors. The German people living in the French, British and American sectors worked so hard at loading and unloading hundreds of aircraft every day, playing a vital role. No doubt their efforts were spurred on by the thought of failure and having to live under the Russian heel.

My mother had made friends with a German girl, Rosemary and helped her out with food and clothes. Willie and I had made friends with some German boys who lived opposite the compound. We traded sweets and chocolate for prewar toys and a Hitler Youth knife. We had a German woman staying with us for a short period, a reasonably attractive blonde with a two-year old little girl called Monica. I didn't think too much about it at the time but what was my mother thinking!

Boys and bullets, boys and guns, potentially deadly combinations! With so many building's still just piles of rubble and remembering the desperate defense of the City, it was inevitable that playing in the ruins,

children would find things that they shouldn't be playing with. The primary finding being ammunition! Any time you moved stuff in a bombed out building you found some ordnance. The bigger stuff did frighten me but regular 303 type bullets were considered to be child's play. We would prise open the casings and collect the gunpowder. When we had what we considered to be enough, we would lay a trail of the powder, from one location to another. Hiding behind something we would light the powder with a match. No explosion of course but great fun.

My father kept his service revolver in the liquor cabinet. Sometimes he would play cops and robbers letting Willie or I hold the gun. It was very heavy and I needed two hands just to hold it in a very unsteady fashion. It was not loaded of course. One day, Willie and I are playing in the house with Mum and Dad sitting next-door listening to the radio. I opened the cabinet where my father kept the gun. Seeing it lying there in its holster, I had a sudden impulse to pull the trigger. The gun was pointing away from me and into a corner. The noise deafened Willie and I and we sat there on the floor in shock. Father came running through in a panic with my mother a pace behind him. Once the smoke literally had cleared, the maid and my mother stopped crying, the post mortem began.

I expected to get a real hiding but I didn't. The shock of the incident apparently was enough of a punishment along with a strong lecture. The bullet had circled inside the cabinet a number of times before burying itself into the wall behind. Apart from our safety, my father's main concern was how to account for the missing bullet. I could have gone across the street and got him a dozen, but I wasn't about to say so!

My father and mother both smoked. Both had taken to using cigarette holders! Smoking never really appealed to me but I certainly was intrigued by the holders. One rainy day sitting in the house with only the maid looking after us, Willie and I decided to try a cigarette. We sat in the front room like a couple of young gentlemen, play acting, each with a lit cigarette and puffing away to our hearts content. The door opened quietly as Mum and Dad entered the room. Busted!

I figured we might be in for a smacking but instead they both burst out laughing. After a minute my Dad, having turned serious, said that if we wanted to be real smokers we should try a cigar! He went to the cabinet and pulled out a cigar, cut it in half, giving a piece to each of us. We were surprised, wondering what was going on and kind of smiling at each other. The smiling stopped, at least on my part, when after lighting the cigar we started puffing. Two inhales and I was done, straight to the bathroom. Willie however seemed to take it in stride and remained a smoker all his life!

Writing about this now and thinking about the near slum we lived in at Millgate Loan, my parents must have thought they had died and gone to heaven. Electric light, indoor plumbing and an elevator! A life where we had a liquor cabinet, fully stocked, a cigarette box always available on the coffee table and a maid to help with the mundane tasks, how good could it get? How quickly we all adapted.

At age nine I knew nothing of the 1936 Berlin Olympics. One of the favorite places that Willie and I would gravitate to was the Olympic Stadium. It had been secured but there were no real fences or barriers, you could just walk right in and we did! Two little boys running around on the soccer field, being cheered on by thousands of fans, in our mind's anyway. I did play on that field. I did imagine all kinds of events and triumphs had I known then the history of this stadium, I would have been in awe.

Underneath the stadium were hundreds of rooms with books, models and all kinds of exhibition material. Seeing film of those 1936 games with Hitler grimacing as Jesse Owens made a mockery of his master race theory makes me think of Willie. Hitler could never have foreseen ten years later two little boys running around in the middle of that huge derelict stadium, scoring imaginary goals for Scotland. We would shout at the top of our voices and listen to the echo resounding through the vast, empty concrete arena.

For some reason unknown to me we moved to Frankfurt after two years in Berlin. Frankfurt am Main was in the American part of Germany, no Russians, no checkpoints, total freedom to go anywhere at any time. We no longer had large accommodations or a maid. A two bedroom flat with four flats to a block was a bit of a comedown. Frankfurt was different from Berlin, you would not think there had ever been a war there, the evidence was so hard to find. There were no bombed buildings anywhere close to where we lived and the general population seemed happy enough. No more compound, no need to take a taxi to school, everything seemed normal.

We had access to all the facilities that the American forces had, AFN (American Forces Network) was THE radio station and in fact our next door neighbor was an announcer on AFN, Ted Norwood. Ted had been a movie producer in Hollywood prior to the war. The PX and the soda fountain were only three blocks away from where we lived, heaven. There were so many different branches of the American forces there that like Joseph; I turned a jacket of mine into a coat of many colors by sewing all the different badges that I could get onto the back of that jacket.

To have to leave this privileged life and return to war torn Britain must have been something that both my parents dreaded. The change we had moving from Berlin to Frankfurt was nothing compared to what was to come. In late 1949, back to Arbroath, with rationing, coal fires, scarcity of everything, dull and almost slum like living conditions! No electric light, no more own room, no central heating or car. Back to reality with a vengeance but my life had already been changed.

Friends & Girlfriends

Like most everyone else my earliest friends were all kids who lived really close by and invariably whom I went to school with. Once at school you find your level and your friends.

Parkhouse wasn't that a great memory for me. My best pals were Drew Chrichton and Dave Smith. They lived up by the "dammy" which was quite far away from where I lived. Back then it was almost in the country. We would play football in the big open fields where Wardykes is now situated but the biggest thrill was baiting the bull that was kept in a small field of its own. This was often a race for life or limb. Run like hell for the fence or the wall. Stepping in pancakes of crap on the way, splattered all up our socks and legs. We all wore short pants and socks then. The farmer used to threaten us every time he caught us. Pants torn on the barbed wire was a pretty common occurrence but the excitement of the chase and knowing you had won was worth it. I think the bull liked it as well.

Football was a great way to make pals it was a very strong bond for most of us. In Germany we had no organized soccer or even any informal games we were too excited with all the stuff going on around us. My friends were limited to the kids whose father's jobs were similar to my fathers. I managed to have a couple of friends, John Brandwood and Lynne Bain.

John was from Manchester and Lynne was from Kirkcaldy. My most vivid memory of John was when we were climbing the compound fence and he slipped, one of the wooden spikes pierced his arm. He was screaming and I was frightened. I had never seen blood and yellow fat coming out of hole in some ones arm before. I helped him off the fence and took him home. That's John with his spiked arm in a sling.

Lynne palled around with my brother and I as there were very few girls for her to play with and of course she was a Scot and that made things that much easier. We were kind of like brothers and sister as we were always together. Ice-skating in the winter on the flooded tennis courts beside our house was a favorite pastime. Of course we were at the age of curiosity, my first sexual experience. I showed her mine and she showed me hers. I thought football and bombed buildings were a lot more exciting.

Back in Arbroath and school at Ladyloan I did make a lot of new friends and the nice part about it was that we all went to the High School together, although not all in the same class. I was picked for the school team and the Arbroath Schoolboys so I got to meet and know kids from all the other schools. Roy and Ian Matthew, Ian and Hugh Nelson, Jimmy Smith, Bill Jarrett, all signed as professionals for English and Scottish teams. Our most humiliating experience was a trip to Methil, in the schoolboy's cup. The bus trip turned out to be the best part. Those kids were like giants compared to us and beat us 9 to 1! Sandy Spink, our goalkeeper was devastated; I couldn't get him to even smile. Come on, 9 to 1, that's not a defeat it's a joke!

A 'headie' friend of mine, Bill Fairweather, lived around the corner from Dave Brown's grain store. The big wooden door of the storeroom was about the same size as a regular full size goal. Bill Brown, the Dundee goalkeeper was there a lot and I used to play 'headie' against him. He was a really nice friendly guy. Eventually he went to Tottenham Hotspur, where he won two FA Cup & League doubles, a European Cup and 23 Scotland "caps."

In the summer the Scottish Football Association, used to run coaching schools for kids. Ours was held at Gayfield and we had a number of the Dundee players, Doug Cowie, Tommy Gallagher, both Scottish Internationalists, helping out with the coaching. The main coaches were Reggie Smith and Reuben Bennett who both later found fame at Liverpool. It was great I got up in the morning and almost ran to the ground. I couldn't wait to get started. In the final game of the three weeks session I scored four goals, I was sure they would sign me on the schoolboy form. The "S" form was not to be, my dreams were shattered when Reggie uttered the words "yir a bra player laddie but yir ower wee."

Somehow in life you tend to remember the failures much more than the successes. In that vein, I think of the two Watters Cup finals that I played in. A short, optimistic walk along Millgate Loan towards Gayfield determined to give of my best. Freshly "dubbined" boots with brand new white laces, dreaming of scoring the winning goal while playing in front of friends and family, I could hardly wait. Reality prevailed, a dismal walk home, full of tears and thoughts of what might have been.

Football was all I thought about until I discovered girls. I liked them and they liked me. My first was a girl on holiday. More experienced in matters of the heart and everything else for that matter, I thought I would die when Rena Davidson, left on the Glasgow train, two weeks of puppy love over but not forgotten.

Intercourse was a dream. Good girls didn't do IT and if they let you get close and then turned you down they were called PT's, a "prick tease." Talk of sex was not at all open. You would have thought that storks really did bring babies, because nobody ever fessed up to having sex. How I was supposed to learn about the "birds and the bees" was beyond me. If you listened to tales of other boy's experiences it was only more confusing and I certainly couldn't ask my mum about it. Safe sex was an oxymoron.

Men and boys carried "FL's" or "slickers," slang names for condoms. It was adjudged a sign of manhood and a good if unworthy application of the Boy Scouts motto, "Be Prepared." You couldn't get condoms out of a machine you actually had to go into a chemist's shop and ask for them. As most assistants in these shops were girls or women it took more than bravado to enter and ask. Jokes abounded regarding questions that might be asked while attempting a purchase. I was totally unaware that one size truly did fit all. I carried one in my wallet for 2 years. A thin, shiny blue packet, its contents worn and rotted with age was finally dispatched to the garbage. The only action it ever saw was in my mind.

Every senior class year has at least one! The girl who is hot and is willing to share, God bless them. I'm not going to tell you who the "hottie" was for me but I still think kindly of her. Although meeting her today I do wonder what all the commotion was about.

My girlfriends in a rough sequence were, Fiona, Leslie, Cynthia, Helen and Jean. In retrospect it was all pretty innocent but it was also a lot of fun.

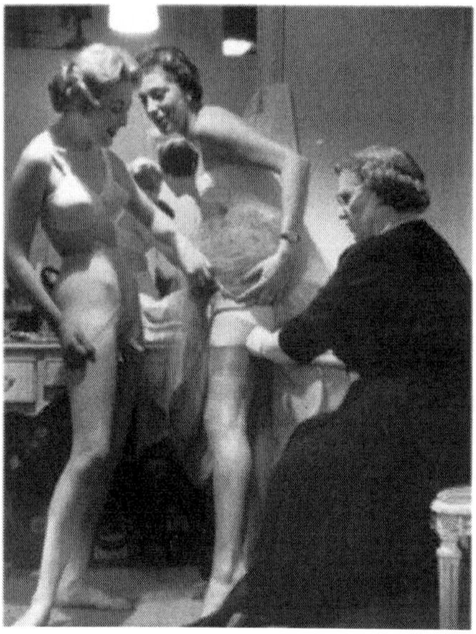

Parents were very protective of their daughters. The best place for any kind of intimacy was the back row of the pictures. One of the few times in my life when I couldn't tell you what the picture was about. A young buck like me had money to spend, remember those tips that I keep mentioning?

Saturday night was THE night for the pictures but more than that, it was a way of showing everyone else that you had a girlfriend. At 15, going to the pictures on your own was a sure sign of immaturity, poor hygiene, shortage of funds or God forbid that you were "queer."

I don't recall any other term than shag" for the act of intercourse. The "f" word was THE swear word but used much less frequently than today. A "feel" was still a "feel" and a flash of stocking tops and knickers, was about as good as you could expect. My limited experience determined that white was the only color of underwear that girls wore. Blue was the most popular color for the dreaded passion killers, ETB's, elastic top and bottoms! Girls and women all wore stockings, there was no such thing as pantyhose .

Stockings and suspenders were a great source of pleasure to all boys of my age, erotica for the generation of men before me and after me. Full chested girls were always popular but those that were, invariably tried to hide the fact. I guess nutrition played a role but the girl with a large bust was a rarity. This observation was not based on personal experience but purely on sight you understand!

What to Do

When schooling was over you had to choose what you wanted to do! Local firms were very anxious to land the latest group of school leaver's who had already completed the basics of technical training. Part of the curriculum was metalwork, woodwork, engineering drawing, mathematics and science. There was no real choice apart from the fact that you could apply for an apprenticeship with one of the local firms. To this end, mini tours of a number of these firms were arranged to provide you with some insight as to what they did. These tours provided thought for furthering your education as well as for learning a skill that would last all your working life.

The retiral ceremony, pictured every week in the Guide and Herald, when a clock and a cheque for a hundred pounds presented after forty years of service, loomed large in my mind! The only thing those tours did for me was to make me want to run. Dirty dark buildings full of noise, men watching the clock and few happy faces. The factories still used leather belts to drive the machinery and the mills were full of dust and loud clacking looms. No thank you.

How could you expect a fifteen-year old kid to make a rational decision? Parents had little to offer as input apart from the fact that they wanted things to be better for their children than they were for them.

Things were changing fast and who really knew enough to advise you. Life experience for most parents was severely limited. Family pressure particularly for the eldest boy, was strong, your income was needed. Money now, was the prime motivator! The only life most boys knew was their home life and the lives of their friends who were all in the same boat.

I had traveled and I had seen how things could be but I knew I wasn't equipped to go out and get them. It was clear to me that I needed to do something different. At fifteen you don't know very much, so guidance is essential. I had no father at home, my mother was still trying to come to grips with all the changes in her life, and I really didn't know what to do. I was not encouraged to leave home but I knew I wasn't staying in Arbroath.

Apart from the 3 comics that I religiously read every week I also used to buy the monthly magazine "Flight," an engineering magazine about the aircraft industry and new aircraft. It was an expensive magazine, 2 shillings and sixpence per month! This was a strain on my tips but for some reason still unknown to me, flying and aviation drew me like nothing else. Faced with the hypothetical choice of being a professional footballer or a fighter pilot, flying would have won.

At the back of the magazine were advertisements for various positions in the aircraft industry. There was no way I could get in even at the lowest level, as I was just 15. I did find an avenue that looked promising though. An advertisement for young school leaver's who wanted to join the Boys Service of the Royal Air Force! When I read that, I was already flying at 30,000 feet testing the latest and greatest aircraft in the world.

The RAF was in dire need of new recruits. WWII had been over for 8 years but Korea and numerous other hot spots had sprung up and required trained personnel for jet aircraft, aircrew and ground crew. The draft or National Service was in force but this only provided a short term solution to the shortage of skilled manpower.

The Boy's Service had been in existence since the early 1930's and was a program that provided technical training for boys aged between fifteen and a half and seventeen and a half, providing you signed on for a minimum of twelve years' service! Your contract didn't begin until you were 18 so you would be 30 when it expired. The purpose was to provide the RAF with a steady stream of young, trained technicians who would eventually become the senior NCO's who would be the backbone of the service. I did not have to be sold, where do I sign?

Going from fifteen years of age to thirty years of age was too much of a jump for my imagination. At thirty you were old, ancient. This seemed so far away that it was quite beyond me but I loved the thought of seeing the world. Meeting interesting people, having a regular job and when 18 years old a chance at pilot training, what more could I ask for? All of these things came true apart from pilot training where my eyesight failed me at the first hurdle.

I don't remember ever asking or talking to any of my classmates about joining up every one of them went in to the apprentice program except Sy. He was asked to stay on at school until he was eighteen and further his education, I was pleased for him, not just because he was my friend but because he was by far the smartest guy in the class.

A number of my classmates joined the Merchant Navy after completing their apprenticeships; almost all became tradesmen in one discipline or another from Electricians to Draftsmen or furthered their education to become Chemists or Engineers. My cousin Percy stayed on at school, got his degree and entered the nuclear power industry, a field that he has spent his whole life in. The only ways for us lesser mortals to gain a degree was to take a job until you were 18 then apply to a University. I don't know anyone in my class that was able to do that. There was no Open University then.

One other route was to attend evening classes at a local college and gain a National Diploma. The time frame for an Ordinary National Certificate was 3 years and a further 2 years for your Higher National Certificate. Not easy to do when you worked full time or you had gotten married. However, out of my class of twenty, most took that route.

After leaving school I worked at Mathieson's grocery store at the foot of the West Port. I stayed for six months until I was fifteen and a half. That was the youngest age that you could be accepted for entry into the Boys Service. The days dragged I felt that my life was on hold. Cleaning up the shop, stocking the shelves and all the time looking at the large wall mounted clock directly across the street from the shop. George my employer encouraged me to go and better myself. On the odd occasion when I look at my Service Record book, I always smile when I see "Grocers Assistant" written as my position before joining up.

Royal Air Force

I never regretted joining the Boys Service. The training gave me knowledge, confidence and a sense of discipline, factors, which provided me with the means to earn a good living to this very day.

Having passed the entrance exams the reality hit that I would be leaving home on my own and everything was going to be new to me, me and fifty nine other fellows that is! My mother was not too keen for me to go but it had always been my goal to get away and be self-sufficient. Flying and aircraft had always been things that I was interested in. Leaving on the evening train from Arbroath was an exciting and scary experience. I knew right then, that the next time I came back home I would be a different person. That knowledge made me feel a little bit of an outsider, even before I left.

I joined the 20th Entry at RAF Cosford, after taking the oath of allegiance to the King! The forms had not been changed yet to read Queen. We were a sorry looking lot, little ones, big ones, white ones and two black kids. I was still small, right on five feet tall but I wasn't the smallest! That distinction fell to two kids from Liverpool who shared a first name, Gary, Minshall and Gary Mountain. I'd never heard of "scousers" before, just the beginning of my education. It took about one hour to make this mob of kids start to look like some kind of group. The loss of hair and civilian clothes equated to a loss of identity.

Kids of my age and older were expected to grow but the uniforms were a pretty good fit as were the boots. Seems like it took me a long time to get over boots! My old school adage of keeping a low profile worked really well through basic training. I managed to avoid "volunteering" for a number of undesirable tasks.

I was designated as an Electrical/Instrument fitter. In 1953 there was no such thing as solid-state electronics or any other kind. A digital display meant showing a certain number of fingers. Aircraft instruments were mainly mechanical devices using vacuum, gyroscopes, springs or optics to register their readings. Instruments were just starting to be combined to form systems. Electrical systems were also pretty basic, DC systems mainly, no small motors or anything like that. The only other group of "sparky" types were the Radio/Radar fitters who were trained primarily on thermionic valves or, as they are better known, tubes.

We lived in wooden huts, like you see in those POW movies; a stove in the middle of the room was the sole source of heating. Beds were arranged down each of the long walls of the "billet." It was important to be close to the stove for heat but you didn't want to be too close for the obvious reasons of fire and also having to keep it going! Beds close to the stove were where you congregated for playing cards or just talking.

Snap inspections were the order of the day, you did not want to have too many of anything and you didn't want to be short of anything either! We were issued full sets of kit including large packs, last thing at night you normally cleaned all the kit and stacked it on top of your locker. Invariably after lights out at 10 o'clock a few would not be able to sleep, the laughter would start for no apparent reason and shortly after piles of kit would be sent crashing to the floor as pillows came in from all directions. We really were just kids. In my last week of basic training the Arbroath lifeboat disaster occurred, I was more upset over that than I was over being away from home. One of our drill Sergeants was from Dundee and knowing I was an Arbroath "smokie" he made a special effort to make sure that I was OK.

After basic training, which lasted for eight weeks, we were moved into the two storied brick blocks. They had central heating and shiny wooden floors with much improved toilet facilities. Once in the new facilities, life changed. You had classes all day and every day except Sunday. On Sunday you were paraded and marched to church. The system did change allowing me to leave camp on Saturday afternoons. Of to Wolverhampton I would go to watch the Wolves play in the English 1st Division. They had a number of England players back them, Wright, Williams, Flowers, Wilshaw, Slater and Hancock. I was at the first floodlit match ever played at Molineux when the Hungarian team Honved, were the opposition.

This was the age of National Service, the Draft, when two years' service was mandatory for all males. It was a very unfair system and truly did cause hardship to a number of individuals and families. On the plus side a large number of those who completed their two-year service stayed on for more. There was a much bigger plus for me, when professional sportsmen were called up for service it was a great chance for me and the rest of us average mortals to play alongside them or at least get to know them a little. My memories are of Ron Flowers the Wolves and England player and Brian London the British Heavyweight Champion. Both were PT instructors during my stay at RAF Cosford.

I learned so much, not just about technical things and aircraft but also about people. The money was poor, after deductions for all kinds of things and then sending money home, I would normally have two shillings and six pence a week left for spending. However once eighteen I would earn a man's wage, four pounds a week! What would I do with all that money?

Today, it seems ludicrous to think of a kid aged 15 joining the Air Force. The navy has long had a tradition of enlisting cadets even younger than that. It was a great experience for me. My brother followed me into the service when he was eligible as did one of our old neighbors, Jackie Mc Farlane.

My passing out parade was on the 5th of May 1955, 5/5/55 how can you forget that! Off to the real air force at RAF Pembrey, real jet planes and pilots but that's another story.

……… ah, got to go, here comes the train.

5048869R00076

Printed in Great Britain
by Amazon.co.uk, Ltd.,
Marston Gate.